EXTRAORDINARY RECIPES FROM

SAN DIEGO
CHEF'S TABLE

MARIA DESIDERATA MONTANA
Photography by John Dole

AMERICA'S FINEST CITY

LP

LYONS PRESS
Guilford, Connecticut
An imprint of Globe Pequot Press

Copyright © 2013 Morris Book Publishing, LLC

Lyons Press is an imprint of Globe Pequot Press.

All photography by John Dole unless otherwise noted

Editor: Amy Lyons
Project Editor: Tracee Williams
Text Design: Libby Kingsbury
Layout Artist: Nancy Freeborn

Library of Congress Cataloging-in-Publication Data is available on file.

ISBN 978-0-7627-8878-1

Printed in the United States of America

10 9 8 7 6 5 4 3 2 1

Restaurants and chefs often come and go, and menus are ever-changing. We recommend you call ahead to obtain current information before visiting any of the establishments in this book.

I dedicate this book to my Italian-born mother who
taught me how to be my own chef in the kitchen.
This one's for you!

Contents

Acknowledgments

When I set out to write this book, I was overwhelmed with the support from local chefs and restaurateurs, each who volunteered a special and unique gift to this project. From the fresh catches on their tables to using grass-fed, hormone-free meats and local produce, these culinary leaders are wholly dedicated to our San Diego community and environment. They are soldiers for a more nutritious diet through the use of sustainable, local, and organic practices that truly benefit the health and well-being of our planet through what we eat on our plates. All this without a hint of sacrifice in presentation or taste! Their recipes reflect a higher passion for the look, feel, and taste of every ingredient, balanced perfectly together in a dish that nearly represents fine art. I am continuously impressed with their ability to take the simplest components and combine them together for an awe-inspiring moment, much like a conductor leading individual musicians to produce a harmonious symphony.

It goes without saying that I must also acknowledge the many local suppliers who have dedicated their lives to providing the best the world has to offer. Fishers who use sustainable practices, ensuring the sensitive ecosystem is minimally impacted and populations of all species remain unaltered. Some even go further, specializing in line-caught or harpooning practices to minimize the use of netting that inevitably creates destruction in our precious oceans. To the cattle ranchers who pride themselves on raising livestock free of hormones and antibiotics, fed on natural grasses from large California pastures. To the poultry farmers focused on free-range practices, allowing their fowl to live natural lives, roaming on large ranches in the crisp California air and feeding on vegetable products. And finally to the produce farmers, who pride themselves on organic practices, free of synthetic pesticides and chemical fertilizers.

A sincere thank you goes to photographer John Dole for his constant support, dedication, and strong work ethic. John worked tirelessly, taking the necessary steps to shoot the most beautiful and alluring photos. John is a consummate professional with extraordinary creative and artistic abilities.

Thanks to my wonderful editor, Amy Lyons, and her entire team at Globe Pequot Press for suggesting the project and allowing me the luxury of tasting beautiful food and learning from some of the greatest chefs in San Diego just how to make these unique recipes in my own kitchen. Globe Pequot Press is a truly professional organization that I would love to collaborate with for many years to come.

And finally, a special word of gratitude to my husband, John, and our two children, Lucia and Frank, for their constant support and patience. My love for cooking began long ago in my mother's Italian kitchen, and it has blossomed over the years, from our small college apartment all the way to our beautiful Southern California home. As a daughter, sister, wife, and mother, I have expressed my love through food, and I hope that the following pages will allow others the opportunity to enjoy the craft in much the same way.

Introduction

When Juan Rodriguez Cabrillo sailed his ship into San Diego Bay on September 28, 1542, he observed the native Indians gathering acorns and fresh fruits and vegetables from the local hills and valleys. The visiting Spaniards also noted their excellent hunting and fishing skills. Fast-forward 470 years and not much has changed! San Diego chefs partner with local farmers and meat/seafood purveyors to bring hungry locals the best that nature has to offer. It's a way of life in Southern California, as more and more people look to healthier, more nutritious alternatives for themselves and their families.

The growth of this region has been most significant in the past fifty to sixty years, as World War II established a strong military presence in the area and was followed by a regular influx of non-natives drawn by the moderate climate and proximity to Los Angeles and Mexico. Although the military and agricultural industries have been long established, tourism, research, and manufacturing have become major influences to the local economy.

Consider the year-round mild climate, long stretches of beaches, and major attractions—including San Diego Zoo/Safari Park, SeaWorld, and Old Town State Historic Park, just to name a few. Major universities and high-tech and research/biotechnology companies also add to the entrepreneurial attitude.

With progress comes diversity, and San Diego is a prime example. Spend some time in "America's Finest City," and you will be rewarded with a peek into many different locales integrated into the region. The county spans a mind-boggling forty-five square miles, from the Pacific in the west to Anza Borrego Desert in the east, Marine Camp Pendleton in the north to the Mexican border in the south. Within these borders you will find restaurants located on stunning ocean coastlines, within a bustling marina, packed together in the historic downtown Gaslamp Quarter, tucked away in suburban strip malls, anchored in large resorts and hotels, and sharing space with a winery among rolling vineyards. The local area was built on the agriculture, ranching, and seafood industries and continues to be a significant influence on the restaurant community.

When I first landed in San Diego twenty years ago, I knew I would call this place home and never want to leave. I have been amazed by the explosive growth of new communities throughout the region. But one thing has not changed: the small-town feel, laid-back attitude, and artistic quality of life that flow in stark contrast to the big city just one hundred miles north. Yes, San Diego is the third-largest city in California and one of the top leisure destinations in the world. But you would never suspect this when talking to the residents or dining with locals. We have kept the small-town feel alive.

San Diego is a vivacious and active food community. We are famous for supporting a health-conscious lifestyle, with an abundant supply of fresh and organic products at our fingertips. The attitudes of chefs and diners alike are friendly and laid-back. With its proximity to the Pacific Ocean and Mexican border, San Diego's cuisine is influenced heavily by Spanish and Asian flavors. With many of the chefs trained in traditional French and Mediterranean styles, it is quite common to hear about "fusion" in the local fare. This is quite simply a technique for blending several different flavors and cooking techniques into a new and vibrant style. Whether you choose to eat in a romantic and sun-soaked dining room with some of the best ocean views in the country or feast al fresco on a cozy outdoor patio studded with palm trees, it's the colorful California modern cuisine that will tempt your taste buds with fusions of imaginative textures and flavors. Of course French and Mediterranean styles are also widely used to perfection as well as Hispanic, Asian, Indian, Latin American, African, and Pacific Island influences.

From celebrity chefs and those recognized by the James Beard Foundation, to those who simply just love to cook, these bastions of their trade pride themselves on being ecoconscious, using only sustainable meats and seafood. Restaurants in San Diego are quickly becoming enchanting places to visit, suitable for even the most discerning of palates. In addition chefs like to take advantage of the moderate climate, where fruits and vegetables flourish on local farms year-round. Passionate for serving farm-to-table cuisine, they continue their pursuit of the best local produce only Mother Nature can provide.

MICROCLIMATES

The vast geographic spread of San Diego County creates a somewhat unique local weather pattern, resulting in a variety of climates suitable for different facets of the food industry. Interestingly you can visit each of the microclimate regions within an hour's drive! The Coastal Region has the mildest weather, rarely stepping outside the narrow range of 50°F to 80°F, usually with clear days bookmarked by a layer of marine clouds in early morning and nighttime. Moving east to the Inland Valley, you will see the temperature range widen, as the summers can be hot, and nights, especially in the winter, can approach freezing. A little farther east you'll experience the Mountain Region, with mild summers days and cooler nights. Rain is more likely here, and winters will frequently see snow. When you finally pass to the easternmost Desert Region, the arid climate is polar opposite to its far-western neighbor, with summer daytime temperatures easily passing 100°F with very cool nights. Each region contributes to the year-round supply of local produce, meats, and seafood available at your favorite eatery.

Undoubtedly, local diners are demanding! They want to know where their food is from, ensuring it's nutritious enough for themselves and their families. The slow-food movement is alive and well in this beautiful city, where the majority of chefs strive to preserve traditional and regional cuisines, while continuing to master their craft in a fashion that supports the ecosystem.

Throughout my career as a food writer, I have made an attempt to uncover the hidden gems and best local dining destinations, but it is quite a challenge. At last count there were over two thousand full-service restaurants in the county! It is very common to see chefs move from one location to another and watch restaurants close while others open their doors. This constantly changing environment inspires culinary ingenuity, where the simplest ingredients are reinvented in new, exciting ways.

Choosing the locations for this book was a difficult task, as there are so many incredible examples of culinary excellence. These chefs are varied in their styles and presentation, and their kitchens are scattered throughout the county, ranging from simple to extravagant. One thing is consistent: These chefs are at the top of their game, gaining national attention for their craft. A good example is chef Brian Malarkey, a local icon who gained notoriety as a contestant in Bravo's hit show *Top Chef Miami* and as a celebrity judge on ABC's *The Taste*. Carl Schroeder, chef/owner of MARKET Restaurant + Bar in Del Mar, received numerous nominations from the James Beard Foundation and was crowned 2004 California Chef of the Year by the California Travel Industry Association. He provides the recipe for the wildly popular Local White Sea Bass and Sweet Corn Soufflé. Another James Beard–recognized chef is William Bradley of Addison in the Grand Del Mar Resort, who was a finalist for the 2012 Best Chef Award. Chef Bradley also received the 2010 Grand Chef from Relais & Châteaux and is one of only 160 chefs on five continents to hold this title. He shares the details of his Baked Dover Sole, as well as the luscious Anise-Poached Pears dessert. Robert Hohmann, currently at the helm of 1500 Ocean in the Del Coronado Hotel and a 2012 James Beard nominee for Top 5 Best Chef in the Pacific, shares his Fig and Fennel Salad. The 2010 National Rising Star Chef winner, Jason Knibb of Nine-Ten in the Grand Colonial Hotel, discloses the secret to his Jerk Pork Belly with Black-Eyed Peas, Garnet Yam Puree, and Scotch Bonnet Pepper Jellies. Master Chefs of France inductee Bernard Guillas of the Marine Room reveals the details of his Old Vine Zinfandel Braised Colorado Lamb Osso Buco with Root Vegetables and Preserved Fruit Polenta.

You now have a window into some of their most favorite dishes, scaled to a size perfect for your kitchen. You'll also gain a higher appreciation for their passion and drive for perfection. Buon appetito!

333 Pacific

333 North Pacific Street
Oceanside, CA 92054
(760) 433-3333
COHNRESTAURANTS.COM
Owner: Cohn Restaurant Group
Executive Chef: Brian Hyre

Oceanside's 333 Pacific is North County's best upscale dining destination, complete with a breathtaking view of Southern California's shoreline from every seat in the house.

A stellar California coastal menu, composed of a variety of entrees, effectively highlights local seasonal ingredients and wholesome preparations that are executed with meticulous care. "We have a number of purveyors who we source from local farms, and during the summer months we even have a guy who grows special vegetables and herbs just for us," says Executive Chef Brian Hyre. "We're always talking to purveyors to make sure we are getting the best of the best. Sourcing local is better for everyone as well as the environment. It's more nutritious, and it tastes better."

Diners have a variety of options to choose from, including raw bar and sushi offerings, soups, salads, pasta, seafood, steaks, chops, and vegetarian choices. "Professionally I just love taking something from a raw ingredient and transforming it," Chef Hyre says. "I love working with my hands and making something that someone will enjoy. It's just the best feeling. It's a form of artistic expression."

On-the-ball foodies are constantly giving high marks to the lamb sirloin encrusted with black trumpet mushrooms and served with roasted fingerling potatoes and cipollini onions. "I think the lamb sirloin is just unique! I love the mushroom crust, because most people normally do lamb with herbs or rosemary—they go the traditional route," says Chef Hyre. "I've done the mushroom crust with different proteins before, and it just adds a totally new dimension."

The lamb is a tender and flavorful meat that can stand on its own, but if you are looking for a quick and easy sauce, Chef Hyre recommends the basil and mint chimichurri. Simply puree equal parts mint and basil with a pinch of garlic, a dash of cumin, a little olive oil, lemon juice, and salt and pepper.

Black Trumpet Mushroom Encrusted Lamb Sirloin

(SERVES 2)

¼ cup dried black trumpet mushrooms
¼ cup all-purpose flour
2 (8-ounce) portions lamb sirloin
Salt and pepper to taste
5 fingerling potatoes
2 teaspoons olive oil, divided
2 small cipollini onions, quartered
1 tablespoon butter
8 asparagus spears

Preheat oven to 425°F.

Grind the mushrooms in a blender or coffee grinder until they become dust. Combine the mushroom dust with the flour in a shallow dish.

Season the lamb with salt and pepper and dredge in the mushroom-flour mixture. Set aside.

Wash and pat dry the potatoes. Place potatoes on a baking sheet and coat with 1 teaspoon olive oil, salt, and pepper. Roast potatoes in the preheated oven until tender, about 15 minutes.

In a sauté pan caramelize onions in butter on low heat (substitute olive oil for the butter if you wish). Remove onions from pan and keep warm.

In the same pan as the onions, sear lamb on all sides. Place lamb in a roasting pan and cook in the oven until the temperature of the lamb is 120°F for medium-rare. Allow the lamb to rest 5 minutes before slicing.

While the lamb is resting, sauté the asparagus in 1 teaspoon of olive oil until al dente.

Slice lamb across the grain and arrange neatly on the plate. Arrange potatoes and onions around the lamb and place asparagus on top.

1500 Ocean

Hotel del Coronado
1500 Orange Avenue
Coronado, CA 92118
(619) 522-8490
HOTELDEL.COM
Chef de Cuisine: Robert Hohmann

A bold-flavored cuisine in conjunction with elegant service, a comfortable but sophisticated ambiance, complete with breathtaking views of the Pacific, makes dining at 1500 Ocean a truly unforgettable experience.

Born and raised in Staten Island, New York, by Sicilian and German parents, Chef de Cuisine Robert Hohmann was constantly in the kitchen making sauces and pasta with his Sicilian grandmother. "I always loved to eat, so it was natural to want to learn how to cook," he says. "Also, my German side had bakers in our family for generations."

A graduate of the French Culinary Institute and backed by an impressive fifteen-year career, Chef Hohmann has worked under the tutelage of a veritable who's who of the culinary industry's greatest chefs, including Jonathan Benno, Mario Batali, Jacques Pepin, and Thomas Keller.

Most of Chef Hohmann's recipes are a combination of the skills he's learned through his career and the culture he was raised in. "I believe in teaching and leading by example. I want my team to feel like they've learned and accomplished something special every day," he says. "I want our guests to feel as if they would not be able to get this kind of stellar experience at any other restaurant."

Chef Hohmann's vision is to take California Coastal ingredients to create the contemporary Mediterranean flavors of Italy, France, and Morocco. He uses fresh produce, herbs, and vegetables from a beautiful on-site garden, as well as local produce and fish from local farmers and purveyors. A favorite among diners, Chef Hohmann's Fig and

Fennel Salad is a bold and flavorful dish that combines figs marinated in a syrup made of port wine and sugar, fennel marinated in olive oil and champagne vinegar, Point Reyes blue cheese, fennel fronds, and Italian black anise seeds.

Chef Hohmann believes that eating everything in moderation is key, using olive oil instead of butter and seasoning food with vinegar instead of salt. He recommends shopping at farmers' markets and buying from local purveyors. "Last thing, do your homework and read labels," he says. "If you don't know what the ingredients are, don't eat it!"

When he's not eating healthy, Chef Hohmann's guilty pleasures are ice cream, root beer floats, and fried chicken.

CORONADO

Situated immediately west of downtown across the San Diego Bay, Coronado is a picturesque destination for any occasion. First established as a resort town in the late 1800s, the most easily recognized landmark is the Hotel del Coronado, a distinctive architectural wonder that has been featured in many films. Although originally accessible only by a ten-mile-long isthmus from the south, Coronado has become a convenient stopover via a tall and curving two-mile-long bridge that connects directly with downtown. The peninsula is also home to a US naval base and training facilities first established during World War II.

Given its coastal location with stunning views of the Pacific Ocean to the west and San Diego Bay to the east, Coronado has a high concentration of restaurants for every palette. Many are within walking distance of the Coronado Ferry Landing, a waterfront shopping/dining area connected to downtown San Diego via a smooth and scenic thirty-minute ferry ride.

Fig & Fennel Salad
(SERVES 8)

For the fig-chocolate sauce:

1 cup port wine
1¼ cups vegetable, chicken, or veal stock
10 figs, cut into quarters
1 double shot espresso
⅛ cup bittersweet chocolate, pieces or chopped
½ stick butter, softened
Sherry vinegar to taste

For the port syrup:

2 cups port wine
1 cup granulated sugar

For the fennel salad shocking oil:

8 cups good-quality olive oil
2 star anise (available in any good-quality
    supermarket or spice shop)
¼ cup fennel seeds
4 heads fennel bulb, each cut into 6 wedges
    (24 pieces total)
Champagne vinegar to taste
Salt to taste

To finish:

8 figs, sliced into quarters
½ pound Point Reyes blue cheese (cubed)
24 fennel fronds, tops only
¼ teaspoon Italian black anise seeds

To make the fig-chocolate sauce: In a large-bottom stockpot combine port wine, stock, and figs. Cook on medium heat until most of the liquid is gone (almost a dry pan, but do not burn). Remove from heat before the pot is completely out of liquid. Add espresso and transfer mixture to a blender. Blend the mixture; while the blender is running, add chocolate and butter and blend until thoroughly combined. When finished blending, add sherry vinegar.

Place sauce in a plastic container with the lid off and cool in the refrigerator. Cover when cool.

To make the port syrup: In a small saucepan, combine port wine and sugar. Simmer over medium heat and reduce until mixture resembles a syrup. Pour into a small bowl and refrigerate until cool.

To make the fennel salad shocking oil: Pour the oil into a large bowl and place in the freezer for at least an hour; let it get as cold as possible without freezing.

Place the star anise and fennel seeds in a small pan and cook on the stovetop over medium heat until the seeds begin to give off an aromatic scent, about a minute or so. Set aside.

Bring a medium pot of salted water to boil. Blanch fennel bulbs in the boiling water until tender. Shock the fennel directly into the cold marinating oil for just a few seconds. Immediately remove the fennel from the oil and place in a bowl. Season with champagne vinegar and salt.

Note: The remaining seeds can be eaten on the salad or discarded, and the oil can be saved and re-used for any other salad dressings.

To assemble: Place the fig quarters in a large bowl and dress with the port syrup and fennel oil. Gently toss figs to coat.

Smear 1 tablespoon of fig-chocolate syrup onto each serving plate. Arrange 3 fennel wedges on top of the sauce. Arrange 4 fig quarters on each plate between the fennel wedges. Then add 4 or 5 blue cheese cubes. Top each salad with 3 fennel fronds and sprinkle just a few anise seeds to complete the plate.

ACQUA AL 2

322 FIFTH AVENUE
SAN DIEGO, CA 92101
(619) 230-0382
ACQUAAL2.COM
EXECUTIVE CHEF: MARTIN GONZALEZ

After attending the Instituto Culinario Apicius culinary school and working as a chef of the namesake eatery in Florence, Italy, Executive Chef Martin Gonzalez returned home to open Acqua Al 2 in downtown San Diego's Gaslamp Quarter in September 2000. Over the years he's built a strong reputation in the community, so it's no surprise that he is the primary caterer for the San Diego Padres, serving their postgame meals during home games.

The Tuscan cuisine is presented much in the same way as it is in Florence, allowing guests to experience all the pleasures of eating at a restaurant in Italy without the expensive plane fare. A casual, yet fine dining atmosphere, the decor is dramatic and rich with brickwork, dark woods, and romantic candlelit tables. With a newly opened third location in the Washington DC area, there is an opportunity to enjoy his menu concept no matter what coast you visit or call home.

Chef Gonzalez and his team offer warm and friendly service paired with exquisite Tuscan cuisine, complete with a diverse selection of wines from Italy and California, as well as their own label of Sangiovese wine. Offering a variety of fresh salads, pastas, seafood, meats, and desserts, the passion that Chef Gonzalez creates in his flavorful dishes is truly unsurpassed. "The style of my cuisine is quite simple," he says, "I create great food using top-quality ingredients, most of which are imported from Italy. This includes the flour I use to make the pastas."

Providing freshness over fuss, the Maccheroni alla Vodka is a perfect example of a traditional Italian dish that Chef Gonzalez is proud to create for his guests. Penne pasta combined with mozzarella, a touch of tomato paste, vodka, milk, and Parmesan cheese proves that a few simple ingredients can result in the tastiest of dishes!

Maccheroni alla Vodka

(SERVES 4)

1 pound penne pasta

1 tablespoon salt

2 ounces fresh mozzarella, sliced into ½-inch cubes

½ teaspoon tomato paste

½ cup (4 ounces) milk

Salt and pepper to taste

1 ounce vodka

¼ cup (2 ounces) Parmesan cheese, grated

Fill a medium saucepan three-quarters full with water and bring to a boil. Add the pasta and salt and stir often to ensure pasta does not stick to the pan. Cook for approximately 6 minutes, or 2 minutes less than directed on the package. Remove the pasta, drain, and rinse under cold water. Set aside.

In a 12-inch sauté pan, combine fresh mozzarella cubes, tomato paste, milk, salt, and pepper and bring to a boil. When the mozzarella is melted (approximately 3 minutes), add the cooked pasta and continue cooking until sauce is reduced (approximately 2 minutes). Add the vodka and let alcohol evaporate (approximately 30 seconds). Finish by adding the Parmesan cheese. Stir well, serve warm, and enjoy!

ADDISON

THE GRAND DEL MAR
5200 GRAND DEL MAR WAY
SAN DIEGO, CA 92130
(858) 314-1900
ADDISONDELMAR.COM
EXECUTIVE CHEF: WILLIAM BRADLEY

Elegant and sophisticated with an opulent yet understated European charm, Addison at the Grand Del Mar continually receives destination-dining recognition and industry awards.

Softly lit with tables that are widely spaced, this Mediterranean-influenced restaurant boasts a massive limestone fireplace imported from Italy, a centrally located wine room, and a handcrafted wood bar topped with stone. Floor-to-ceiling arched windows overlook magnificent views of the lush garden landscape and the eighteenth hole of the Grand Golf Club.

Executive Chef William Bradley and his team offer a unique, memorable dining experience by delivering the highest level of haute cuisine. "We have a winning team in the kitchen and at the front of the house, all with a strong commitment to culinary excellence," he says. "We constantly up the ante for ourselves year after year by differentiating our tasting menus, always challenging ourselves to learn more about food and wine, expanding our wine program, mentoring new staff members, and pleasing new and returning guests in every way we can."

When cooking gourmet food, Chef Bradley believes that all preparation and dishes must be driven by flavor. Therefore the only option is to use the very best ingredients—and these great ingredients always stem from the local farmers. Chef Bradley's recipes for Anise-Poached Pears and Baked Dover Sole with Lemon-Lime Jam & Fines Herbes are near and dear to his heart because they are simple, yet flavorful. "I do feel that I have an extremely refined palate, a gift that life has given to me," he explains. "I also feel that over the years and through experience, I've come to understand that less is more."

Chef Bradley feels he is more than a cook, but a mentor, decision-maker, and friend on many levels to his fellow colleagues. He is also grateful for wonderful opportunities to travel to remarkable places and meet unique and interesting individuals.

ANISE-POACHED PEARS

(SERVES 4)

10 anise seeds, toasted
4 large Bosc pears, peeled (see Chef's Tip)
4 cups Sambuca liqueur
2 cups water
1 cup granulated sugar

In a small sauté pan, toast anise seeds over low heat to release the oils; set aside. Place pears in a heavy-duty saucepan. Cover with Sambuca liqueur, water, sugar, and toasted anise seeds. Cook over low heat for 1 hour, turning over each pear every 10 minutes.

Place each pear into an individual plastic container and pour syrup over the top. Place the lids on the containers and refrigerate for 48 hours. This will allow the pears to macerate and pick up all the individual flavors.

These pears are great sliced on top of a salad or served as a dessert course or as an accompaniment to a main course. Be creative!

Chef's Tip: This recipe also works well with apples.

Baked Dover Sole with Lemon-Lime Jam & Fines Herbes

(SERVES 4)

For the lemon-lime jam:

6 whole lemons, peeled, seeded, and cut in half
6 whole limes, peeled, seeded, and cut in half
4 cups lemon sparkling water
3 cups organic cane sugar
¼ cup fresh diced ginger

For the sole:

4 (4-ounce) Dover sole fillets
Fleur de sel (sea salt) to taste
¾ cup salted French butter (room temperature)

For garnish:

2 leaves each fines herbes for garnish
(tarragon, chives, chervil, and parsley)
4 tablespoons extra-virgin olive oil
Fleur de sel (sea salt) to taste

To make the lemon-lime jam: In a heavy-duty saucepan over low heat, add lemons, limes, sparkling water, sugar, and ginger. Cook uncovered for 1 hour, stirring occasionally.

To make the sole: Preheat oven to 200°F. Season each fillet of sole with sea salt. In a large piping bag, add the tempered butter and pipe over each individual fillet until completely coated. Bake sole in preheated oven for 8 minutes, then remove and let stand for 5 minutes.

To plate: On each serving plate, place a fillet of sole and arrange fines herbes on top of each; spoon over olive oil and sprinkle with sea salt. Place a small dollop of Lemon-Lime Jam on the side.

Alchemy Cultural Fare & Cocktails

1503 30th Street
San Diego, CA 92102
(619) 255-0616
ALCHEMYSANDIEGO.COM
Executive Chef: Ricardo Heredia

Alchemy is a vibrant and energetic neighborhood eatery committed to providing local sustainable food while displaying a passion for the arts and the community. With art pieces rotating every six weeks and a menu that changes seasonally, adventurous guests like to return time and time again. "We like to welcome everyone into our home, so our regular customers feel like they are just as much a part of Alchemy as we are," says Executive Chef Ricardo Heredia.

Chef Heredia began cooking at the age of nine in his own home. Over the years he has worked in a number of kitchens, learning culinary styles spanning countries such as Italy, France, Thailand, and the Caribbean. He says he is a natural-born cook in the flavor business, using freshly picked produce at its peak. "I feel that supporting local farmers is a duty, not only as a chef, but as a member of our community. The closer my products are to me, the faster they land on the plate."

Drawing from the inspirations of his youth, Chef Heredia is also an avid volunteer at the Albert Einstein Academies Student Chefs Program, where he can educate young minds on the importance of local and sustainable ingredients. He feels his passion for learning led to a passion for teaching, which has helped him define his true identity in the kitchen today.

Popular favorites on Alchemy's menu include handmade Pretzels with Beer Mustard, Local White Sea Bass with Caramelized Fennel, and Cranberry Bread Pudding with Ginger Caramel, Buttermilk Gelato, and Toasted Pumpkin Seeds. "The pretzels have been one of my favorite foods since I was a child. I loved rolling them out. It's very simple, yet complex in technique and repetition, which taught me a valuable lesson in the kitchen." The pretzels are also one of those must-have items that will never leave Chef Heredia's menu, regardless of the season.

Pretzels with Beer Mustard

(YIELDS 8 LARGE PRETZELS)

For the pretzels:

3 cups warm water (110°F–115°F) water
2 tablespoons granulated sugar
4 teaspoons kosher salt
2 tablespoons active dry yeast
5 cups bread flour
1 stick (4 ounces) unsalted butter, melted
2 tablespoons baking soda
2 cups water
2 large egg yolks beaten with 1 tablespoon water
Course sea salt, for sprinkling

For the beer mustard (yields 2 cups):

½ cup yellow mustard seed
1 cup brown mustard seed
2 tablespoons brown sugar
2 tablespoons salt
1 cup water
1½ cups pilsner (pale lager beer)
¾ cup champagne vinegar

To make the pretzels: Combine water, sugar, and kosher salt in the bowl of a mixer and sprinkle the yeast on top. Allow to sit for 5 minutes or until the mixture begins to foam. Add the flour and butter and, using the paddle attachment, mix on low speed until well combined. Change to medium speed and knead until the dough is smooth and pulls away from the side of the bowl, approximately 4 to 5 minutes.

Move the dough to a large bowl, cover with plastic wrap, and let sit in a warm place for approximately 50 to 55 minutes or until the dough has doubled in size.

Preheat oven to 400°F. Line a cookie sheet with parchment paper and spray with cooking spray. Set aside.

Turn the dough out onto a lightly floured work surface and divide into 8-even pieces. Roll out each piece of dough into a 30-inch rope. Make a U-shape with the rope and then, holding the ends of the rope, cross them over each other and press onto the bottom of the U in order to form the shape of a pretzel. Place onto the parchment-lined cookie sheet.

Combine baking soda and water in a spray bottle and shake well. Spray the pretzels with the mixture to cover. Partially pre-bake the pretzels in the preheated oven for approximately 5 to 8 minutes, until they start to brown. Remove from the oven and cool on a rack.

To finish, brush the top of each pretzel with the beaten egg yolk and water mixture and sprinkle with course sea salt. Return to the baking sheet and bake until dark golden brown in color, approximately 10 minutes more.

To make the mustard: Roughly grind yellow and brown mustard seeds or crush with a mortar and pestle. Combine ground seeds with remaining ingredients in a saucepan. Cook on low for 45 minutes, stirring occasionally. Remove from heat, transfer to a bowl, and allow to cool in refrigerator. Serve with pretzels.

A.R. Valentien

The Lodge at Torrey Pines
11480 North Torrey Pines Road
La Jolla, CA 92037
(858) 777-6635
arvalentien.com
Executive Chef: Jeff Jackson

Executive Chef Jeff Jackson says that at this point in his career, it's all about passing on the knowledge. "When I lived in Chicago in the early 1980s, I was fortunate enough to work for a mad Frenchman who taught me how to cook really well, out of fear!" he says. "It wasn't personal, it was just his passion. I used to cry myself to work, but I learned what a true passion for cooking was all about."

Chef Jackson feels comfortable and at home at A.R. Valentien, located inside the Lodge at Torrey Pines and wants all his dining guests to feel the same way. "This is not like a hotel to me, it's more like a large residence. If it's small, it's manageable. A monster hotel wouldn't allow me the freedom I need."

Dedicated to working directly with local farmers, Chef Jackson changes the menu daily, based on what is fresh and seasonal. "The farmer grows it and the chefs cook it. Whatever produce comes in, we will use. My staff and I play with the food. We taste it and talk about it. We are always thinking about what would be best to eat," he explains. "I don't go to work, I go to play. I rely on the creative process for my day-to-day existence."

Chef Jackson's philosophy evolves around simplicity, and he takes an Italian standpoint when it comes to cooking, believing that less is more. "Don't mess with the ingredients, and allow the food to maintain its integrity," he says. Since he loves cooked lettuce, Chef Jackson believes that grilling romaine gives the outside of the lettuce a smoky flavor, while the inside remains crisp. His Alaskan Halibut with Barigoule Vegetables is rich and flavorful, yet light and easy to make and perfect for any occasion year round.

Grilled Romaine with Prosciutto & Burrata

(SERVES 6)

For the anchovy vinaigrette:

2 shallots, minced
6 cloves garlic, sliced very thin
½ cup young balsamic vinegar
Pinch salt
1 cup extra-virgin olive oil
10 white anchovies, chopped
Fresh ground pepper
¼ cup chopped parsley

For the romaine:

6 romaine hearts
4 fresh burrata cheese chunks (5–6 ounces each)
12 slices prosciutto di Parma
Salt and pepper to taste
¼ cup vegetable oil

To make the vinaigrette: In a large bowl, macerate the shallots and garlic in the vinegar with salt for about 5 minutes. Whisk in the olive oil and anchovies. Season with a turn of the pepper mill. Add the parsley just before serving.

To make the romaine: Wash the romaine hearts thoroughly and dry on paper towels. Split each in half lengthwise.

Cut each burrata into three equal pieces. Carefully lift up several of the inside leaves of romaine and tuck a piece of the cheese inside.

Wrap each romaine half with a slice of prosciutto, ensuring that the area where the burrata resides is well covered and sealed. Lightly season the romaine with salt and pepper and brush lightly with oil.

Prepare a grill or barbecue to medium-high heat and cook the romaine on all sides and place on a warm platter. Dress with Anchovy Vinaigrette and serve.

Alaskan Halibut with Barigoule Vegetables

(SERVES 2)

For the barigoule sachet:

1 bay leaf
15 basil leaves
1 sprig thyme
10 peppercorns
1 (8-inch) square cheesecloth
4 inches butcher string

For the barigoule vegetables:

1 small leek, whites only
1 shallot
1 celery rib
3 pearl onions
4 baby carrots
4 baby parsnips
2 baby fennel
⅔ cup olive oil
1¼ cups white wine
1½ cups chicken stock
8 baby artichokes
Salt to taste

For the halibut fillets:

2 (6-ounce) Alaskan halibut fillets
2 ounces grape seed oil
Salt and white pepper to taste

To make the barigoule sachet: Place all the ingredients in the center of the cheesecloth. Bring the corners together and tie off with the butcher string.

To make the barigoule vegetables: Split and wash the white part of leek. Slice the leek into ⅛-inch slices.

Slice the shallot into ⅛-inch slices. Wash and slice the celery into ⅛-inch slices. Peal the pearl onions. Trim tops off of and scrub the carrots and parsnips.

In a nonreactive pot (with lid) warm the olive oil over medium heat. Add all the vegetables except the artichokes and cook for 10 minutes. Add wine and reduce by half. Add chicken stock, artichokes, and sachet. Season with salt, cover pot, and reduce heat to low. Once artichokes are tender to the point of a knife, remove the pot from heat. When the artichokes are cool enough to handle, cut them in half and return to the broth. Remove and discard sachet.

To make the halibut fillets: Preheat oven to 350°F.

Season the halibut fillets with salt and white pepper. Place a 10-inch frying pan over high heat and add the grape seed oil. Once the oil is hot, add the halibut fillets and sear until brown on both sides.

Remove fillets from heat. Transfer the fillets and barigoule vegetables to a baking dish and place in the oven. Cook for 4 minutes and baste with the barigoule broth. Cook 5 minutes more or until cooked through.

Ave 5 Restaurant & Bar

2760 5th Avenue
San Diego, CA 92103
(619) 542-0394
avenue5restaurant.com
Chef de Cuisine/Co-Owner: Colin MacLaggan

Hard work and dedication, coordinated with an evolving cuisine, have kept diners coming back time and time again to this exclusive restaurant and bar, based in San Diego's Bankers Hill District.

As a child, European-trained San Diego native Chef Colin MacLaggan enjoyed preparing food alongside the family matriarchs in preparation for their regular dinners together. He never thought of cooking as a chore, but rather as a fun and wonderful experience where he could bond with family and friends.

Serving progressive American fare with a mix of French food and modern techniques, Chef MacLaggan says his "middle of the road cuisine" can be can dressed up or down. "We wanted a kind of modern cafe type feel with great food, progressive music, and surreal art—a place where guests can get a great 'fine dining' meal and not get cold stares from the next table for laughing too loud," he says. "My close friends and family come visit me more often, since I basically live here."

Known for their monthly changing menu with nightly specials and an award-winning Sunday brunch, Chef MacLaggan relies on sustainable, local, and organic ingredients, believing it's more cost-effective and healthy. "In Italy it's always been a way of life. I have to laugh when restaurants use this as a 'new' selling point to consumers, because most good chefs have been cooking this way their entire careers," he explains. "If chefs didn't commit to this way of cooking at the start, they missed the boat."

Chef MacLaggan's Pear Chutney is a sweet and versatile appetizer, perfect as an accompaniment with assorted cured meats and cheeses, with wild game, or as a simple dessert paired with a crusty baguette or served on top of your favorite ice cream.

PEAR CHUTNEY

(MAKES 3 CUPS)

1 cup peeled and grated apple

½ teaspoon salt

½ cup peeled, seeded, and chopped tomatoes

⅓ cup minced onion

⅓ cup chopped dry prunes

1 tablespoon orange zest

Juice of 3 oranges

1 cup granulated sugar

¼ teaspoon ground cinnamon

¼ teaspoon ground nutmeg

¼ teaspoon cayenne

1½ tablespoons minced ginger

1 cup champagne vinegar

Pinch saffron

¾ pound pears, peeled, cored, and diced into large chunks

Combine all ingredients except pears in a large saucepan and bring to a boil. Reduce heat to low and, stirring every 10 minutes, simmer mixture until thick and jamlike, approximately 30 minutes. Add pears and continue stirring every 10 minutes, simmering mixture gently on low heat, until pears are just cooked, about 30 minutes more. Remove from heat and let cool to room temperature. Store any unused portion in a covered container in the refrigerator.

BALI HAI RESTAURANT

2230 SHELTER ISLAND DRIVE
SAN DIEGO, CA 92106
(619) 222-1181
BALIHAIRESTAURANT.COM
CO-OWNERS: LARRY AND SUSIE BAUMANN

Known for its gorgeous location on Shelter Island with magnificent views of the San Diego Bay marina and city skyline, Bali Hai has been an independent family owned favorite for nearly sixty years. Mr. Bali Hai, a large wood sculpture at the front entrance, greets guests while "The Goof," a playful and mysterious remnant, stands guard on the roof. There is also a private dock on the property, allowing boaters to conveniently drop by and dine.

The Polynesian interior boasts natural materials, including grassy and bamboo wall coverings and flooring. Bali Hai also has an extensive collection of Polynesian artifacts, including tiki figures, statues, antique tapa cloths, wood weapons, ocean charts, maps, and native pictures that decorate the entire restaurant. Other interior additions include a private dining room upstairs, a resort-style lounge featuring a backlit honey onyx bar, and classic-style Hawaiian light fixtures over the bar and staircase to create a soft, romantic glow. It is also an extremely popular choice for weddings and receptions, combining breathtaking views and festive cuisine.

The Pacific Rim–inspired menu takes advantage of the wide variety of farm-fresh regional ingredients available, focusing on a seasonal and approachable cuisine. The culinary team works diligently to create light dishes that emphasize the different aspects of the palate, including hot, sour, salty, and sweet. Creative chefs experiment with different types of Asian cuisines, taking a collaborative approach and fostering new dish concepts together. This unique strategy allows each chef a greater sense of ownership in what he or she creates and cooks every day.

The Sansho Rubbed Swordfish with Soba Noodle Salad combines some great classic Asian flavors, including the Szechuan peppercorns, warm soba noodle salad, and orange sesame dressing, for a palate-pleasing dish. It is part of the restaurant's Kai ("the Sea") offerings for dinner and remains one of their most popular dishes with multiple generations of patrons.

Sansho (Szechuan Pepper) Rubbed Swordfish with Soba Noodle Salad

(SERVES 4)

For the sansho rub:

1 tablespoon Szechuan peppercorns
½ tablespoon black peppercorns
½ tablespoon coriander seed
½ tablespoon fennel seed
½ tablespoon kosher salt

For the soba noodle dressing:

¼ cup soy sauce
½ teaspoon sesame oil
¼ cup rice vinegar
½ teaspoon Sambal
1 tablespoon garlic, chopped
½ cup granulated sugar
1 tablespoon water
1 tablespoon cornstarch

For the orange sesame vinaigrette:

¼ cup orange juice reduction (found at stores)
1 teaspoon sesame oil
½ tablespoon tamari
½ tablespoon honey
¼ cup olive oil and canola oil blend
    (substitute extra-virgin olive oil if desired)
Salt and white pepper, to taste
Micro greens (red micro shiso for color), for garnish

For the soba noodle salad:

4 ounces dry soba cha (green tea) noodles
    (found in a Japanese market, or the Japanese
    section of a grocery store
¼ cup julienned carrots
¼ cup seeded and julienned red bell pepper
¼ cup peeled and julienned red onion
¼ cup mung bean sprouts
¼ cup thinly sliced scallions

For the swordfish:

4 (5-ounce) swordfish steaks
Black sesame seeds and toasted white sesame seeds,
    for garnish (can be store bought individually)

To make the sansho rub: Toast the peppercorns, coriander seed, and fennel seed in a frying pan over medium heat, about 1 minute. Transfer to a coffee grinder and grind until fine. Remove to a bowl and add salt.

To make the soba noodle dressing: Combine all the ingredients except water and cornstarch in a small saucepan and bring to a boil. While the mixture is heating up, combine the water and cornstarch in a small bowl to create a slurry. Once the dressing has come to a boil, slowly drizzle the slurry over it and whisk until the dressing is thick enough to coat the back of a spoon.

To make the orange sesame vinaigrette: Combine orange juice reduction, sesame oil, tamari, and honey in a bender. While the blender is running, slowly drizzle in the oil blend to emulsify. Add salt and white pepper.

To make the soba noodle salad: Toss all the ingredients with the soba noodle dressing to coat.

To make the swordfish: Rub swordfish with the sansho rub and char grill over hot coals until just cooked through, about 3 minutes per side (depending on thickness of steaks).

To plate: Place a small amount of the soba noodle salad in the center of each serving bowl and then set one piece of swordfish on top. Drizzle the orange sesame vinaigrette around the bowl and sprinkle black and toasted white sesame seeds on top of the vinaigrette. Garnish the top of the vinaigrette with micro greens (red micro shiso for color).

Bencotto Italian Kitchen

750 West Fir Street
San Diego, CA 92101
(619) 450-4786
lovebencotto.com
Owners: Guido Nistri and Valentina Di Pietro
Chef: Fabrizio Cavallini

Bencotto means and refers to a meal "done well," or perfectly cooked. In Bencotto's kitchen, culinary expertise meets the highest quality and genuine taste.

Created by a husband-and-wife team from Northern Italy, Guido Nistri and Valentina Di Pietro, with the support of Chef Fabrizio Cavallini, the concept of Bencotto was conceived as a natural extension of the depth and breadth of Italy's culinary heritage. The founders' core belief is that high-quality food can be simple and supremely delicious. With an American as well as international audience in mind, Bencotto came to life inspired by the authenticity of an Italian kitchen juxtaposed with modern scenery.

Combining their range of experiences from the restaurant business in Milano, Modena, San Diego, and New York, the philosophy at Bencotto is that food can be made simple and supremely delicious and that everything on the menu is prepared fresh and made to order. The owners' unique approach to Italian cooking tradition offers

handmade "home-style" dishes in an environment that reflects who they are—a young generation of Italians who celebrate their culinary heritage, presented in a modern, relaxed, and inviting kitchen-restaurant.

Located in the Little Italy community of San Diego, Bencotto's space is designed to welcome guests as they enter an inviting contemporary Italian family kitchen with warm Old World service. Contemporary and modern, this two-story restaurant is nothing short of chic and sophisticated, complete with high ceilings, glass, and natural exposed concrete on the floor and walls. "The atmosphere and ambiance is a combination of Milan, where we were born and raised, and New York City, where we lived for awhile," says Di Pietro.

Bencotto is the ultimate Italian eating experience, drawing inspiration from the kitchens where Italians grow up, cook, and eat. From fifteen kinds of handmade pasta to organic olive oil, delicious soups and salads, and hormone-free chicken, a designed-to-share layout encourages diners to casually pick and choose from an assortment of exquisite homemade dishes. "We like to keep it very simple, using only three ingredients per dish at the most," says Di Pietro.

A tasty appetizer with a delicate flavor, the Tortino di Cavolfiore (Cauliflower Soufflé) is best eaten alone, but it also pairs nicely with any meat or fish.

Tortino di Cavolfiore

Cauliflower Soufflé

(SERVES 8)

1 head cauliflower
2 cups milk
1 cup cream
¾ cup fresh ricotta
1 cup grated Parmesan cheese
3 large eggs
⅔ cup all-purpose flour
8 small ramekins
Nonstick cooking spray

Clean the cauliflower and remove the stems and core.

In a large pot, cook the cauliflower with the milk and cream. Simmer the over low heat until tender, about 30 minutes. With a strainer, separate the milk and cream and save only the cooked cauliflower.

Put the cooked cauliflower in a food processor or blender and add the ricotta, Parmesan cheese, eggs, and flour. Blend just until smooth.

Preheat oven to 350°F.

Spray the bottom of eight small ramekins with nonstick cooking spray. Spoon the cauliflower mixture into the ramekins and bake for 30 to 45 minutes. The Tortino di Cavolfiore should be golden brown on top and a toothpick inserted in the middle should come out clean.

BICE

425 ISLAND AVENUE
SAN DIEGO, CA 92101
(619) 239-2423
BICESANDIEGO.COM
EXECUTIVE CHEF: MARIO CASSINERI

Born and raised in Milan, Italy, Executive Chef Mario Cassineri has created a menu that he himself would like to see at a fine dining Italian restaurant. And since BICE (Bee-chay) is all about traditional Italian dishes and culture, Chef Cassineri likes to teach people how to properly appreciate cheeses by pairing them with myriad special marmalades, honey, wine, and crackers. The salumi and cheese bar is a wondrous site, located directly inside the open dining room with wall-to-ceiling windows accentuating natural light.

Passionate about authenticity and cooking the Italian way, Chef Cassineri prides himself on offering new and unique food creations incorporated with sustainable, local, and organic products. "I never cover up the taste of anything with heavy condiments or

cream," he says. "I like to keep all ingredients in their freshest and simplest form." As for eating out, Chef Cassineri believes it is very important to go for traditional cuisine. "Go to an American restaurant for American food and go to a Mexican restaurant for Mexican food. Never go to a place that mixes a great number of cultures or flavors together."

Popular favorites among the guests include Chef Cassineri's Branzino on Cedar Plank, Pistachio Tart, and his Classic Ragu Bolognese that he makes from scratch. Chef Cassineri shares this popular recipe with a flavorful combination of ground beef, pork, and veal and porcini mushrooms that provide a smoky aroma. "A good cook needs to do the traditional, popular dishes well before he or she can master other dishes," he explains. "The secret is to be a team leader; the team has to work together with knowledge and passion."

The aspect of Mario's career that gives him the most satisfaction is being recognized as a great chef and food creator. He believes it's his patience that has made him the success he is today.

Classic Ragu Bolognese

(SERVES 4–6)

2 tablespoons extra-virgin olive oil

1 garlic clove, minced

1½ cups chopped onion

1½ cups chopped celery

¾ cup chopped carrots

6 ounces lean beef, coarsely ground

6 ounces lean veal, coarsely ground

3 ounces lean pork, coarsely ground

½ cup red wine

½ cup canned crushed tomatoes

2 tablespoons tomato paste

1 cup water

1 ounce dry porcini mushrooms, soaked in
    hot water and pureed in a blender

Salt and pepper to taste

1 tablespoon unsalted butter

1 pound pasta (your favorite kind), cooked
    according to package directions

Heat the olive oil in a large, heavy saucepan over medium-high heat. Add the garlic, onion, celery, and carrots and sauté until golden in color. Add the beef, veal, and pork, breaking up mixture with a wooden spoon, and continue stirring until meat is cooked through. Add red wine and boil for a couple of minutes.

Add the tomatoes, tomato paste, water, and pureed porcini mushroom mixture and season with salt and pepper. Reduce heat to very low and gently simmer, covered, stirring occasionally until all the flavors meld, about 1½ hours. Add the butter and give the mixture another good stir. Serve over your favorite pasta.

BlueFire Grill

La Costa Resort and Spa
2100 Costa del Mar Road
Carlsbad, CA 92009
(760) 929-6306
lacosta.com
Chef de Cuisine: Gregory Frey Jr.

Several fabulous options are offered inside the BlueFire Grill at La Costa Resort and Spa, including a traditional dining room experience with plush booths and a fireplace, or guests can choose to be in the center of all the action with the exhibition kitchen. The lounge is a cooler, trendier space with a glass bottle fireplace that changes color and an outdoor plaza patio that is perfect for appetizers and drinks.

From meat and seafood to produce, oils, and even jams, Chef de Cuisine Gregory Frey Jr. is dedicated to using fresh local products. "I believe in the continuing progress in the development of our local food culture, while still keeping a close tie to the traditional methods that we have built this restaurant upon," he says. "The Baja Ceviche was the first item I added to the menu at BlueFire Grill, and it has been a big success. I feel this dish encompasses exactly what we are all about, and almost all of the ingredients are found right here in our own backyard. My cooking is all about being fresh and responsible."

Chef Frey likes to use sustainable, local, and organic ingredients, not because it's fashionable, but because it's the way he was taught. "It feeds my passion. There is always someone growing something new, and these people are more interested in getting the ingredients to be the best they can be, the way nature intended," he says. "We choose our ingredients here based on flavor most importantly, not on a shelf life or price."

Chef Frey is enthusiastic about all things food, and making sense of pure chaos is where he derives the most fun in his job and why he loves working in the restaurant business. His passion keeps him motivated and provides the joy that makes being a chef more of a lifestyle than a career.

Baja Ceviche

(SERVES 6–8)

1 pound Baja bay scallops, cleaned

½ pound Baja pink shrimp, cut into large dice

1 pound Baja halibut fillet, cut into ¾-inch cubes

1½ cups fresh lime juice, divided

1 avocado, diced into ½-inch cubes

Salt and pepper to taste

½ cup Pacific stone crab meat (optional)

1 cup Persian cucumbers, sliced into ¼-inch rounds

1 cup tangerines or oranges, peeled, seeded, and pulled into segments

½ cup fresh cilantro, finely chopped

½ cup extra-virgin olive oil

1 tablespoon Mae Ploy sweet and sour sauce (available at most grocery stores or Asian markets)

Your favorite tortilla chips

Soak scallops and shrimp in 1 cup lime juice in the refrigerator overnight in a covered bowl. Soak the halibut in ¼ cup lime juice in the refrigerator for 4 to 5 hours in a covered bowl.

In a small bowl, mash the avocado with a spoon until chunky. Add 2 teaspoons lime juice and season with salt and pepper. Set aside.

Drain the scallops, shrimp, and halibut and place in a large bowl. Add crab (if using), cucumbers, tangerines or oranges, cilantro, and olive oil. Season with 1 to 2 tablespoons lime juice, Mae Ploy, salt, and pepper.

Place the avocado on a serving plate and top with the seafood ceviche. Serve with your favorite chips.

Blueprint Cafe

1805 Newton Avenue
San Diego, CA 92113
(619) 233-7010
BLUEPRINT-CAFE.COM
Owner/Chef: Gayle Covner

Catering to the downtown businessperson looking for an alternative to Hispanic cuisine, Blueprint Cafe offers made-from-scratch lunch fare prepared quickly. The emphasis is on seasonal, natural, and familiar presentations, better known as comfort food. Clearly a hit with the local businesses, the cafe is packed during the lunch hours every workday, with the vibe extending across a large radius of the usually sleepy neighborhood.

Owner and Chef Gayle Covner has been at the helm of In Good Taste Catering for twenty-nine years, which housed a large, well-lit kitchen in the East Village area of downtown San Diego. When City College expanded in the original building, she relocated

south to Barrio Logan and designed and built her catering kitchen in the rear of Mark Steele's architectural firm. Hence Blueprint Cafe became the name of the restaurant. Offering indoor and outdoor dining, the interior is a bold statement that complements the building's host, with bright colors and artwork meant to excite the senses. This is the perfect place to sip a warm cup of coffee or tea and savor mouthwatering edibles in an upscale environment.

Covner thinks of her urban eatery as friendly, colorful, and accessible, not trendy or scary. After forty years of cooking, she is patient, creative, and technically proficient. From creating delicious soups of the day, including Manhattan Clam Chowder or Tomato and Basil, to specials of Grilled Mahi Mahi with Honey Glaze or Slow Cooked Pulled Pork BBQ on a kaiser roll with shoestring fries, Covner says, "I am a teacher. I like to play with food and I love all the best bites of everything."

For the sweetest of desserts, Covner has been making her well-known Chocolate Chip Brownies for a Crowd for thirty years. With a few simple ingredients, the recipe is easy to make and the brownies taste fudgy and never cakey. "These brownies get better with age!" she says.

CHOCOLATE CHIP BROWNIES FOR A CROWD

(YIELDS 30 BROWNIES)

2¼ cup butter
2⅔ cups semisweet chocolate chips
12 eggs
5 cups granulated sugar
1 tablespoon vanilla
4 cups all-purpose flour, sifted
1½ teaspoons salt

Preheat oven to 350°F.

Spray a 12 x 17-inch cookie sheet with nonstick cooking spray and a light dusting of all-purpose flour. In a saucepan on low heat, melt the butter and chocolate chips; set aside.

In a large bowl, beat the eggs and sugar (don't make it bubbly with air). Add the vanilla and melted chocolate and mix and stir. Add flour and salt, a little at a time, gently stirring after each addition; don't overmix. Pour batter on cookie sheet and bake for 35 minutes. Allow to cool before cutting into squares.

BO-beau Kitchen + Bar

4996 West Point Loma Boulevard
San Diego, CA 92107
(619) 224-2884
COHNRESTAURANTS.COM
Executive Chef: Katherine Humphus

A destination restaurant with a neighborhood feel, this casual bistro is reminiscent of a cottage in a tiny village in the south of France, with two dining rooms and a bar and outdoor patio complete with a stone fireplace. The stone walls reflect natural light by day and the warm glow from antique fixtures at night, adding to the ambiance.

A graduate from Le Cordon Bleu, Paris, France, in 2009 with a Le Grand Diplome in Cuisine and Pastry, Executive Chef Katherine Humphus cares about using sustainable, local, and organic ingredients. She prefers to source most of her products from Specialty Produce and local farms, namely Point Loma Farms, as often as possible. Her menu is filled with classic dishes, but the ingredients and presentation are quite modern and approachable.

Handling the art of multitasking while understanding the difference and importance of time restraints, quality, and perfectionism, Chef Humphus says she enjoys seeing the immediate reaction from smiling faces after enjoying her cuisine. "Much to my surprise, I'm also actually really loving the training aspect of being a chef and teaching other young minds new techniques."

Chef Humphus credits her parents for their support and her grandmother for keeping her engaged in the kitchen—helping her understand that cooking is fun and creative. She believes people should exercise portion control, even more so than the types of food they are eating. "Everything in moderation," she says. "Lemon juice, mustard, and fresh herbs have almost no calories and can make anything taste good!"

The Peanut Butter Brittle recipe she shares is a sugary and distinctive dessert that's quick and easy to prepare at home. "It's a real show-stopper at the restaurant," says Chef Humphus. "It's so good, we actually have to hide it from the other employees!"

PEANUT BUTTER BRITTLE

(SERVES 12–15)

1½ cups granulated sugar
1½ cups corn syrup
¼ cup water
2 tablespoons butter
2 cups raw peanuts
1 teaspoon soda water
2 teaspoons water
1 teaspoon vanilla extract
2 cups peanut butter
Candy thermometer
Nonstick baking mat (available at any
    cooking/supply store)

Combine sugar, corn syrup, and water in a large saucepan and insert a candy thermometer. Bring mixture to a boil and, stirring occasionally, cook mixture until it reaches 275°F.

Remove candy thermometer and stir in butter. Lower heat to medium and add the peanuts. Stir for 5 minutes and cook until candy starts to turn brown and re-inserted candy thermometer reads 300°F.

Add soda water and stir. Remove candy mixture from heat and stir in vanilla. Then lightly stir in the peanut butter.

Pour the candy onto a nonstick baking mat placed on a baking sheet and spread out thin with a spatula. Let cool before breaking.

Cafe 222

222 Island Avenue
San Diego, CA 92101
(619) 236-9902
cafe222.com
Chef/Proprietor: Terryl Gavre

Serving fun versions of American breakfast fare since 1992, Cafe 222 has gained popularity with both locals and tourists alike, which has been the key to its longevity. First opened in a redevelopment area of San Diego's Marina District, the industrial-influenced cafe now sits in the middle of a large residential district, making it a favorite destination for breakfast or lunch. The long lines of patrons waiting for their chance to savor their favorite dish are a testament to the consistency and quality of the menu.

Upbeat and quirky with a bright and sunny ambiance, chef and proprietor Terryl Gavre doesn't consider herself to be a "chef," but loves food, cooking, and being around chefs. "My eatery is a fine-tuned little buzzing machine that has a great staff and rocks it out every day," she says. "I don't think I have any special talents in the kitchen that any experienced home cook doesn't have. I think a person just has to love cooking and be willing to work like a dog in order to do it for a living."

Popular favorites at Cafe 222 include the Buttery Scones and Pumpkin Waffles, which Chef Gavre says are very easy to make at home. "The waffle is a moist and spice cake-like waffle. It is wonderful with just butter and a little bit of syrup. It's also great with fresh whipped cream and a little sprinkle of grated fresh nutmeg on top."

Chef Gavre is a big believer in eating healthy at home and just "going for it" when she goes out. "I usually roast a ton of vegetables on the weekend, add a little salt and pepper, and eat them for lunch all week. I also drink a big fruit and vegetable smoothie every morning for breakfast. After being good all day, I feel like I can pretty much eat what I want at dinner, which includes dining out."

PUMPKIN WAFFLES

(MAKES 6–8 WAFFLES)

2½ cups all-purpose flour

¼ cup brown sugar

1 tablespoon baking powder

½ teaspoon cinnamon

1 teaspoon ground ginger

¾ teaspoon salt

¼ teaspoon ground cloves

4 large eggs

2 cups whole milk

1 cup fresh or canned pumpkin puree

Splash vanilla extract

¼ cup melted butter

In a large bowl combine flour, sugar, baking powder, cinnamon, ginger, salt, and cloves. Sift fingers through the dry ingredients to break up any brown sugar lumps.

Add eggs, milk, pumpkin, and vanilla; mix well. Fold the butter in last and mix only until smooth. Prepare waffles according to manufacturers' instructions on your waffle iron.

Buttery Scones
(YIELDS 8–10 SCONES)

2½ cups all-purpose flour

½ cup granulated sugar

1 tablespoon baking powder

½ teaspoon cream of tartar

2 teaspoons grated lemon or orange zest

1½ sticks butter, well chilled or frozen,
    cut into cubes

½ cup heavy cream

¼ cup buttermilk

Course ground sugar, for dusting

Your favorite fruit, jam, or nuts, for garnish

Preheat oven to 400°F.

Place flour, sugar, baking powder, cream of tartar, and lemon or orange zest in a large bowl. With a fork, gently mix to combine. Using a pastry blender, combine butter with the dry ingredients until mixture resembles the texture of oatmeal.

In a small spouted pitcher or measuring cup, combine heavy cream and buttermilk. Slowly add the wet mixture to the dry mixture (you may not need all of the liquid) until just combined. Set aside a bit of the liquid for brushing the scones before baking.

Turn the dough onto a slightly floured surface. Dust your hands with flour and gently knead the dough just enough so that it stays together when you form a ball. Roll out dough into a disk about 1 inch thick. Cut the disk with a cookie or biscuit cutter and place scones on a lightly greased or parchment-lined cookie sheet. Leave about 1½ inches between scones.

Brush the top of each scone with a little of the remaining liquid and sprinkle with course ground sugar. Bake until light golden brown, about 12 to 16 minutes. Garnish with your favorite fruit, jam, or nuts.

CAFE CHLOE

721 9TH AVENUE
SAN DIEGO, CA 92101
(619) 232-3242
CAFECHLOE.COM
EXECUTIVE CHEF: KATIE GREBOW
PROPRIETOR: TAMARA RATLIFFE

This is a bustling cafe in the morning with customers clamoring for cappuccinos, a busy bistro for lunch, and a romantic hideaway complete with music and flickering tea lights by nightfall.

Cafe Chloe provides bistro-style cuisine based on the repertoire of dishes in France, including Coq au Vin, Steak Frites, Frisee au Lardon, Daube d'Agneau, Cassoulet, and Choucroute Carnie. The majority of the produce is purchased from local farms, and the menu is designed around what's fresh and in season. "The food on the menu revolves around what's being harvested," says Executive Chef Katie Grebow. "In addition, we try to make conscious decisions to buy seafood that is sustainable and meats that are raised in regard to slow-food ethics, as in no antibiotics and no hormones."

One of Chef Grebow's specialties, and something that is very near and near to her heart, is cheese. "I consider myself a cheese connoisseur. We've served over five hundred different types of cheese at the cafe," she says. "Being a chef allows me to be creative all day long and work with my hands. Beats desk work for sure."

Chef Grebow's popular quiche recipe is based on ingredients one would find in the Pays Basque region of France. Part of the local cuisine is piperade, which is an egg, pepper, and ham dish. The mixture consists of locally grown peppers in combination with onions, tomatoes, and garlic. It is often finished with a spicy pepper, like pimento d'espellette, and a bit of vinegar. This pepper ragout is combined with local ham and stirred into eggs as they cook in a pan. It is eaten like a frittata, and in this recipe, Chef Grebow has added a quiche crust to make it a little easier to bake and serve.

QUICHE BASQUAISE

(MAKES 1 QUICHE OR SERVES 6–8)

1 red bell pepper, sliced into thin strips

1 yellow bell pepper, sliced into thin strips

½ onion, sliced into half moons

2 Roma tomatoes, seeded and halved

1 tablespoon olive oil

4 garlic cloves, chopped

1 teaspoon vinegar, preferably sherry

3 eggs

¾ cup cream

¾ cup whole milk

½ teaspoon salt

Pinch white pepper

¼ pound prosciutto, sliced and torn into pieces

1 uncooked piecrust (8–9-inch pan)

In a large sauté pan over medium heat, sauté peppers, onions, and tomatoes in olive oil.

Add the garlic to the vegetable mixture. Once they begin to soften, turn the heat to low and simmer vegetables, stirring often, until they get very soft, broken down, and a bit saucy, approximately 10 more minutes. Add the vinegar and set mixture aside to cool.

Preheat oven to 350°F.

In a large bowl whisk the eggs. Add the cream, milk, salt, and pepper; mix well. Add the vegetable mixture and prosciutto to the eggs. Pour into piecrust. Bake quiche for 20 to 30 minutes, until the middle is firm and set.

OLIVE OIL

Did you know that the first olive trees planted in modern America were at the Mission San Diego back in 1789? One of the most essential ingredients in any kitchen, olive oil has long been used for a variety of interesting applications, including in skin and hair care, as a digestive aid, for polishing wood furniture, for lubricating machinery, and even as a shoe polish. But for many centuries civilizations have marveled over its taste and texture in their daily diets. More recently science has garnered proof that this golden liquid has cardiovascular benefits, as it has a high concentration of monounsaturated fat, which is a cholesterol-fighting component of any meal.

If you're looking for the freshest olive oil from a local source, be sure to visit the California Olive Oil Council's website. Here you will find a comprehensive list of certified growers and local supermarkets, fun facts, recipes, and events that focus on this little marvel (cooc.com).

CARNITAS' SNACK SHACK

2632 UNIVERSITY AVENUE
SAN DIEGO, CA 92104
(619) 294-7675
CARNITASSNACKSHACK.COM
OWNER/CHEF: HANIS CAVIN AND SARAH STROUD

Owned and operated by husband-and-wife team Hanis Cavin and Sarah Stroud, Carnitas' Snack Shack is a pork-centric eatery that serves excellent food. "We change a portion of our menu every day and try to utilize as many products as possible from local farmers and artisan cheese and sausage makers," says Chef Cavin. "We have an unassuming façade and I think the quality of our food sometimes surprises people, at first."

Don't let this shack fool you! An outdoor-only dining establishment, the atmosphere is bright and lively, yet laid-back but attentive. Offering elaborate presentations, Chef Cavin is constantly striving to use only sustainable and organic ingredients. "My relationship with local growers and artisan food producers is continuing to expand as I become more known for my food," he says. "Every day I have the chance to create a meal that no one has ever tasted before. I want my guests to feel that they just ate something that was truly memorable."

Popular favorites include the Shack Pork Sandwich with pulled pork, pork schnitzel, and smoked bacon with peperoncini pickle relish, or the Steak Sandwich with shaved prime rib eye, jalapeño-cheddar bread, chipotle aioli, pickled serrano peppers, jalapeño jack cheese, and roasted tomatoes. Additional recipes that are true originals to the shack are the Pork Burger with Candied Bacon and Gorgonzola and the vegetarian-desired Beet Terrine with Balsamic Syrup, with goat cheese, spinach, and drizzled balsamic syrup.

Open since December 2011, the business continues to grow and Chef Cavin is looking to open more locations in the near future. He is extremely proud to be a part of San Diego's food scene. He is heavily involved in youth programs and fundraising efforts throughout the community and city. In addition, he helps local charities by doing what he really loves to do—cook! "Our tastes are always changing and we feel like we are creating history every day at our little San Diego snack shack," says Cavin. "We couldn't be happier."

Beet Terrine with Balsamic Syrup

(SERVES 8)

For the beet terrine:

3 large red beets, peeled and roasted
3 large yellow beets, peeled and roasted
3 cloves garlic
2 cups fresh spinach
8 ounces goat cheese
Salt and pepper to taste

For the balsamic syrup:

2 cups balsamic vinegar
½ cup honey

To make the beet terrine: Preheat oven to 325°F. Clean beets under cool running water and place them in a 9 x 9-inch metal roasting pan with 2 cups water and garlic. Cover with aluminum foil. Roast for 1½ hours or until wooden toothpick comes out clean. Let cool, then peel the skin by rubbing beets with a wet towel. Slice beets into ¼-inch rounds.

In a bread pan, place a layer of beets and then follow with spinach, goat cheese, salt, and pepper; repeat. Finish with a third layer of beets. Place in the refrigerator and allow to chill for 1 hour.

To make the balsamic syrup: Add vinegar to small saucepan and cook over low heat until a quarter of the liquid remains (with a syrupy consistency), approximately 30 minutes. Remove from heat and add honey. Let cool 5 minutes. Place syrup in a plastic squeeze bottle.

To plate: Remove the chilled beet terrine and cut into 3-inch squares. Using a spatula, remove one square at a time and place in the center of small plate. Drizzle syrup over the beet terrine.

Pork Burger with Candied Bacon & Gorgonzola

(SERVES 4)

2 pounds ground pork butt
1 large carrot, finely diced
1 tablespoon minced fresh Italian parsley
1 teaspoon minced garlic
Salt and pepper to taste
1 pound bacon, diced into large chunks
¾ cup brown sugar
4 hamburger buns
1 cup Gorgonzola cheese
Your favorite greens for garnish

Place ground pork in a large bowl with carrots, parsley, and garlic. Add salt and pepper and mix together. Form pork into four patties. Cook in a sauté pan on medium heat for 6 minutes, then turn over and cook for 6 minutes more.

Place bacon and sugar in another large sauté pan and cook until bacon just starts to crisp. Strain fat and cool.

Place each burger in a bun and add some bacon and Gorgonzola. Garnish with greens of your choice.

THE FISH TACO

One of the most widely recognized culinary choices synonymous with San Diego, the fish taco has become a Southwest phenomenon. The combination of beer-battered local fish, shredded cabbage, salsa, and creamy sauce wrapped in a flour tortilla has long been a staple of seaside Mexican taquerias. But it wasn't well recognized until the early 1980s, when a local college student named Ralph Rubio decided to bring the recipe north of the border. The success of his restaurant chain has spurned others into the trend, with different variations of this simple formula available on nearly every street corner, from seaside taco joints to high-end dining rooms. With a wide variety of local seafood and produce available year-round, the flavor combinations are endless! But one thing is certain, this humble recipe is steeped in tradition and will always represent the fusion of cuisines that has made San Diego a culinary hub for the most distinguished of palates.

Casa Guadalajara

4105 Taylor St
San Diego, CA 92110
(619) 295-5111
CASAGUADALAJARA.COM
Owner: Diane Powers
Executive Chef: Jose Duran

Festive and colorful, the atmosphere at Casa Guadalajara features the trademark style of owner Diane Powers, incorporating the warmth and charm of Mexican decor with stunning dining rooms and patios reminiscent of Mexican haciendas. Vintage wooden gates, splashing fountains, and exquisite color-drenched patio dining is made all the more authentic by strolling mariachis.

What sets this beautiful restaurant apart from other restaurants in Old Town can be summed up in one word: authenticity. "We offer fresh Mexican cuisine and unique

decorations from all over Latin America so that our guests feel that they're not just being served a plate of food, but an experience," says Manager Filiberto Horta. "We want everyone to feel he or she has truly been transported south of the border."

Apparent among Executive Chef Jose Duran's many strengths in the kitchen is his impressive continuity. Having been with Casa Guadalajara since the beginning, Chef Duran has kept his trademark cooking style consistent throughout the years, preserving dishes that have been longtime favorites as well as developing new ones and keeping with the same high standards and delicious taste that he has become known for.

"Whenever possible or available, we like to use local and organic ingredients. We try to not just 'live in the present,' so to speak, but to think about the generations after us and how we can help preserve life for them," Horta says. "When we can, we particularly like to buy some of our most-used ingredients, like tortillas and vegetables, from local vendors."

The Mexican Shrimp Cocktail is an iconic coastal favorite that has been a trademark of delicious Mexican cuisine for years. It's a light and refreshing appetizer, perfect for people to make at home if they are hosting a party or dinner. Guests like the "kick," which is a result of the black pepper, horseradish, and Tabasco and Worcestershire sauces.

The Enchiladas de Vegetables Con Queso showcases one of Chef Duran's delicious vegetarian menu options. The combination of fresh vegetables—including squash, zucchini, bell peppers, and spinach—paired with a rich enchilada verde sauce, gives it superior flavor and makes it something even nonvegetarians like to order. Enchiladas are also easy to cook for entire families or large groups of people.

Old Town

Considered the "Birth Place of San Diego," Old Town State Historic Park is located immediately north of downtown. It's an easy drive or trolley ride from many locations. Interestingly, it is one of the most highly visited tourist attractions in all of San Diego, a formidable task in light of the many other destinations within driving distance. Primarily focused on preserving California history, the park includes five of the original adobe buildings, a schoolhouse, a blacksmith's shop, a carriage stable, and a museum. Nearby you can also visit Presidio Park, site of the first European settlement on the US West Coast in 1769, as well as the Heritage Park Victorian Village. Adjacent to the park is a small village that includes a high concentration of border-inspired shops, restaurants, and cantinas. Locals and tourists will agree that it's the best location for Mexican and California cuisine, including flavors that span both traditional and modern influences.

Mexican Shrimp Cocktail

(SERVES 4)

⅓ cup chopped red onion

¼ cup freshly squeezed lime juice

1 pound chilled cooked medium-size shrimp, peeled, deveined, and tails removed

1 cucumber, peeled, seeded, and finely chopped

2 stalks celery, finely diced

2 medium tomatoes, diced

2 teaspoons salt

2 teaspoons ground black pepper

½ cup chilled tomato juice

½ cup chilled Clamato juice

½ cup freshly squeezed orange juice

½ cup chilled ketchup

1 teaspoon horseradish

½ bunch fresh cilantro, stems discarded and leaves chopped

2 tablespoons Worcestershire sauce

2 tablespoons Tabasco sauce

2 avocados, peeled, pitted, and chopped

4 orange wheels, for garnish

4 cilantro sprigs, for garnish

Mix onions with lime juice in a small bowl and allow to rest for 10 minutes.

Meanwhile, toss shrimp, cucumber, celery, tomatoes, salt, and black pepper in a bowl until thoroughly combined.

In a large bowl, whisk together juices, ketchup, horseradish, cilantro, Worcestershire, and Tabasco. Add shrimp mixture and gently fold in avocados. Cover and chill thoroughly, at least 1 hour.

Serve in chilled cocktail glasses and garnish with orange wheels and cilantro sprigs.

ENCHILADAS DE VEGETABLES CON QUESO

(SERVES 6)

1 tablespoon olive oil
½ cup julienned zucchini
½ cup julienned yellow squash
½ cup chopped red onions
½ cup julienned carrots
½ cup diced green bell peppers
¾ cup diced red bell peppers, divided
½ cup fresh spinach, coarsely packed and finely
   chopped
½ cup whole kernel corn
1 teaspoon salt
2 cups canned or jarred enchilada verde sauce, divided
12 (6-inch) corn tortillas
2 cups shredded Monterey Jack cheese
Fresh cilantro leaves, finely chopped, for garnish

Preheat oven to 350°F.

Heat oil in a skillet over medium heat. Add zucchini, squash, red onions, carrots, green peppers, and ½ cup red bell peppers. Cook 5 minutes or until golden brown and tender. Add spinach, corn, and salt. Cook and stir until spinach wilts.

Spread ½ cup enchilada sauce in a 3-quart shallow baking dish. Fill each tortilla with vegetable mixture (about ½ cup each) and Monterey Jack cheese (about 2 tablespoons each) and roll. Place rolled tortillas in prepared baking dish. Spread with remaining enchilada sauce and half of remaining cheese.

Bake 20 minutes. Top with remaining cheese and bake until cheese melts, about 5 minutes more. Serve two enchiladas per plate and garnish with chopped cilantro leaves and remaining diced red bell pepper.

CUCINA URBANA

505 LAUREL STREET
SAN DIEGO, CA 92101
(619) 239-2222
CUCINAURBANA.COM
OWNER: TRACY BORKUM
EXECUTIVE CHEF: JOE MAGNANELLI

In the heart of Banker's Hill, this California-inspired Italian kitchen and wine shop is constantly packed with people chatting, having fun, and enjoying great food and drink with their friends and family.

Successfully providing a value-driven dining experience for all guests, the restaurant's interior evokes a modern kitchen combined with the history and comfort of

an old rustic country farmhouse while embracing the elements of community dining and family-style presentations. "It is our intention to provide incredible food and wine at affordable prices in a very interesting atmosphere," says Executive Chef Joe Magnanelli. "Our commitment to fine-dining service principles has also been a key part of our success."

Through a whimsical expression of Italian classics, Chef Magnanelli is committed to using seasonal, local, and organic ingredients throughout his menu, maintaining strong working relationships with several local farms and purveyors. "Some of my personal favorites are working with whole animals, making homemade pasta, and coming up with dishes that combine the simple authenticity of Italian cuisine with the robust freshness of California ingredients."

While Chef Magnanelli enjoys the creative part of cooking and takes pride in watching guests indulge in his cuisine, he says the relationships he builds with his crew are just as important to him; he especially enjoys watching the progress that his newer team members make every day. He believes strongly in cooking with real and natural ingredients and consuming only whole and unprocessed foods.

The Ricotta Gnudi is a specialty that diners crave at Cucina Urbana on a regular basis. These pasta-like dumplings, made with ricotta cheese and semolina flour, are so soft and pillowlike, they melt in your mouth. Topped with brown butter and shavings from an almond biscotti cookie, this luxurious delicacy will have your dinner guests wondering if you spent hours in the kitchen, when in fact you didn't!

RICOTTA GNUDI

(SERVES 6)

2 pounds whole-milk ricotta cheese
½ cup finely grated Parmesan cheese
    (more for garnish if desired)
Salt and pepper to taste
3 cups semolina flour, divided
4 tablespoons unsalted butter
10 sage leaves
1 almond biscotti

In a large mixer, combine the ricotta cheese, Parmesan cheese, salt, and pepper until you have a smooth and creamy consistency.

Spread a small amount of the semolina flour in a 2-inch-deep, 9 x 13 inch stainless steel or glass pan. Portion out 1 tablespoon balls of the ricotta mixture (gnudi mix) and place on top of the flour. Dust your hands with some of the flour, coat the balls with more flour, and place them back in the pan. Pour the remaining flour over the top of the balls, covering them fully. You should not be able to see the gnudi at all. Cover and keep refrigerated for exactly 24 hours.

After 24 hours, immediately remove the gnudi from the flour and dust most of the remaining flour off. Set aside and keep refrigerated until ready to use.

Bring a large pot of salted water to a boil. In a large sauté pan over high heat, brown the butter and add the sage. Drop the gnudi into the water and cook for just a minute. Remove and set gnudi on a large platter lined with paper towels.

When the butter has just started to become brown, add the gnudi. The butter should "froth." Keep the gnudi moving in the pan for a couple of minutes, turning them over frequently. When they are brown on all sides, they are done. Remove gnudi and place them in a serving bowl. Pour the sage brown butter sauce on top and around.

Finish by grating a small amount of the biscotti over the top of the dish with a Microplane or the fine side of a box grater. Add Parmesan cheese for garnish if desired.

Cups La Jolla

7857 Girard Avenue
La Jolla, CA 92037
(858) 459-2877
cupslj.com
Owner: Michelle Lerach
General Manager: Nina Park-Shin Han

Everyone deserves a sweet treat every now and again! Utilizing an all-organic, three-star green-certified kitchen, Cups specializes in sweet treats for everyone, including gluten-free, dairy-free, vegan, and diabetic options. The atmosphere at this cozy cupcake shop

is inviting and comfortable. There's plenty of room for dessert lovers to sit, relax, and thoroughly enjoy their lattes and cupcakes. "I love creating something that makes at least one person happy," says General Manager Nina Park-Shin Han. "I am really good at coming up with one-of-a-kind flavors!"

A state-of the-art teaching kitchen is on-site, making it a great destination for one of the many classes offered throughout the month or for a special party or team-building gathering. Cups also manages a thriving catering business, especially for birthdays and weddings.

When it comes to her recipes, owner Michelle Lerach likes to think outside the box from a typical cupcake. Her popular Limone Ricotta Cupcakes with Lemon Cream Cheese Frosting aren't something guests would expect to find anywhere else. Lerach uses only choice ingredients that set her cupcake haven apart from other bakeries. She cares about what she puts into each product, making everything from scratch as often as possible, including her lemon sugar and ricotta cheese. "Knowing we use the best ingredients makes me proud," says Park-Shin Han. "Getting to know the farmers who grow the products we use is just icing on the cake."

Park-Shin Han also believes that eating organically encourages people to eat healthier. "If people were to do their grocery shopping in a market that sells primarily organic products, they would be surrounded by grassroots product," she says. "I feel that this is the best way to start cooking healthy meals. Be inspired by what is in season and be adventurous with choices, which will in turn lead to healthier choices and a healthier lifestyle!"

LIMONE RICOTTA CUPS
WITH LEMON CREAM CHEESE FROSTING

(MAKES 2 DOZEN CUPCAKES)

For the cupcakes:

2 cups almond meal or finely ground almond flour
1 cup gluten-free flour blend
2 cups softened butter
3 cups plus 1 tablespoon granulated sugar
4 cups whole milk ricotta cheese
8 eggs
2 teaspoons vanilla extract
Lemon oil to taste

For the frosting:

1¾ cups softened cream cheese
1 cup unsalted butter
½ tablespoon vanilla extract
Pinch salt
¾ cup powdered sugar
1 teaspoon lemon oil

To make the cupcakes: Preheat oven to 350°F.

Sift almond meal or almond flour and gluten-free flour together; set aside. In a large mixing bowl of a stand mixer, cream together the butter and sugar until light and fluffy, making sure to scrape down the sides. Add the ricotta cheese and mix until well combined. Add one egg at a time, mixing well after each addition, until batter is smooth and all eggs are combined. Slowly mix in the flour, stopping periodically to scrape down the sides. Add vanilla and lemon oil.

Scoop mixture into lined cupcake tins about three-quarters full. Put on the middle rack in the oven and bake for about 25 to 30 minutes.

To make the frosting: In a large mixing bowl of a stand mixer, blend the cream cheese and butter until smooth and fluffy. Make sure to scrape down the sides of the bowl. Add the vanilla extract and salt and beat until just combined. Add powdered sugar in two batches until well incorporated. Add lemon oil on low speed until just combined.

Frost cupcakes after they have fully cooled.

Cusp Dining & Drinks

Hotel La Jolla
7955 La Jolla Shores Drive
La Jolla, CA 92037
(858) 551-3620
cusprestaurant.com
Executive Chef: Donald Lockhart

Cusp has the ambiance of a unique seaside dining experience, complete with weathered hardwood floors, petrified wood candle niches enclosed by smoked glass, and wood sculptures that evoke visions of driftwood along the shore.

With an unparalleled city and ocean view from the eleventh floor of the Hotel La Jolla, the entire restaurant is laid out in front of gorgeous picture windows infusing sunlight throughout. The open kitchen invites guests to watch as their dinner is prepared and even, if just a bit, converse with the team. "There is nothing more enjoyable than speaking to guests," says executive chef Donald Lockhart. "They impart a sense of excitement and delight and are the best part of our restaurant."

Chef Lockhart is passionate about high-quality food and driving others to success. He never allows the previous day's "highs and lows" to affect his overall goals and direction in the moment. Through his vast kitchen experiences, Chef Lockhart says that simplicity leads to amazing things. "Over-thought ideas lead to confusing and

unappetizing messes. I have come to believe that thinking simpler and eating a little lighter not only creates a more enjoyable eating experience, but more of a focus on the quality of the ingredients as well."

Lockhart and his team strive by their own standards and ideals, believing in the bettering of a guest's experience through the creation of great tasting and simply prepared food that is classically rooted with a modern twist. He is constantly creating partnerships with local harvesters and artisans who represent the best products the region has to offer. This has produced amazing results, allowing him to develop more inventive cuisine possibilities. Chef Lockhart's passion for cooking with fresh ingredients from California's local bounty has driven him to concoct a unique Stuffed English Cucumber with Toasted Quinoa and Tzatziki appetizer that is simple and elegant and speaks for itself in presentation and flavor.

STUFFED ENGLISH CUCUMBER
WITH TOASTED QUINOA & TZATZIKI
(SERVES 8)

For the filling:

2 English cucumbers, peeled and
    sliced in half lengthwise
1 tablespoon canola oil
½ cup cooked quinoa (add a bit of salt when cooking)
2 tablespoons minced red onions
1 tablespoon chopped cilantro
1 tablespoon chopped parsley
2 teaspoons lemon juice, divided

For the Thai basil tzatziki:

¼ cup plain Greek yogurt
2 teaspoons minced Thai basil
    (available at Asian markets)
1 teaspoon minced cilantro
Juice and zest of 1 lime
¼ teaspoon ground cumin
Salt and pepper to taste

For the topping:

Zest of half a lemon
2 tablespoons extra-virgin olive oil

To make the filling: Using the point of a spoon, remove seeds from cucumber halves, hollowing them out. Set aside.

In a small heated sauté pan, add enough canola oil to lightly coat the pan. Add quinoa and, stirring continuously, toast until golden brown, about 3 to 5 minutes. Remove from heat and cool.

In small bowl, mix together the quinoa, red onions, cilantro, parsley, and 1 teaspoon lemon juice. Set aside.

To make the Thai basil tzatziki: In a medium bowl, gently combine all ingredients except the salt and pepper. Season with salt and pepper to taste.

To make the topping: Mix together 1 teaspoon lemon juice, lemon zest, and olive oil.

To plate: Fill the cavity of each cucumber half with tzatziki and then top with quinoa mixture. Cut the boats into 1-inch pieces. Drizzle with topping.

DALLMANN FINE CHOCOLATES

2670 VIA DE LA VALLE
DEL MAR, CA 92014
(858) 720-1933
DALLMANNCONFECTIONS.COM
OWNER: ISABELLA VALENCIA

The history of Dallmann began in 1954 when Guenther Dallmann opened his pastry shop in St. Gilgen, Austria, offering only three types of pastries that were baked fresh daily. Because of Dallmann's attention to detail and use of supreme ingredients, it didn't take long for his pastry shop to become recognized locally as the ultimate pastry paradise.

Today Guenther's daughter Sylvia, together with her husband Franz, have expanded Dallmann, gaining an international reputation of being one of the best pastry shops around. In 2006, Franz and Sylvia's daughter Isabella Valencia expanded the family business into San Diego, California, opening Dallmann Confections and specializing in exquisite artisan chocolates for the wholesale industry.

Keeping with the family tradition of using only the finest ingredients, Valencia hand

makes Dallmann gourmet chocolates using the original family recipes. In 2011 she opened her first chocolate boutique, Dallmann Fine Chocolates, in Del Mar, offering a variety of chocolate products such as exotic truffles, bars, nuts, and hot cocoa to the real chocolate aficionado. "I'm proud to keep the family tradition alive and well in a different continent, combining our history with a modern twist."

This light and airy chocolate boutique is warm and welcoming with high ceilings and many wood touches. It's a place that Valencia built specifically for people who are passionate about premium quality chocolate and to educate those who are interested in learning. The display case, specifically built to look like a jewelry case, allows plenty of seating room for people during weekly tastings. Her favorite aspect of being a chocolatier is to see the reactions on peoples' faces while they enjoy her confections. "I'm satisfied when a customer tells me that I just made their day. It all makes sense when you see that the joy you give someone is as simple as a piece of chocolate!"

Valencia created the Lavender Sea Salt Truffle because she wants to open people's minds to unusual flavor combinations. "There's nothing better than the pleasant surprise on a person's face when trying an exotic chocolate truffle."

Dallm

FINE CHO

Fig Balsamic

Lavender Sea Salt Truffles

(YIELDS 20 TRUFFLES)

½ tablespoon lavender leaves

1 tablespoon light corn syrup

½ cup heavy cream

1½ cups bittersweet chocolate, chopped fine

Pinch fleur de sel

½ cup Dutch process cocoa powder

1⅓ cups semisweet or bittersweet chocolate,
    finely chopped

In a small saucepan over medium heat, simmer the lavender leaves, corn syrup, and heavy cream. Remove from heat and allow mixture to rest for 15 minutes. Place the 1½ cups bittersweet chocolate in a large bowl.

Heat up the cream mixture again and then, using a strainer (to strain the lavender leaves), pour the mixture over the chocolate and let stand for 2 minutes. Using a rubber spatula, stir gently, starting in the middle of bowl and working in concentric circles until all the chocolate is melted and the mixture is smooth and creamy. Add a pinch of fleur de sel and place in the refrigerator for 2 hours.

Using a melon baller, scoop chocolate onto a cookie sheet lined with parchment paper and return to the refrigerator for 30 minutes.

Place the cocoa powder in a pie pan and set aside.

In the meantime, place the 1⅓ cups semisweet or bittersweet chocolate into a medium-size mixing bowl and melt in the microwave for 30-second intervals until all chocolate is melted.

Remove the truffles from the refrigerator and shape into balls by rolling between the palms of your hands (use powder-free vinyl or latex gloves, if desired). Dip an ice cream scoop into the melted chocolate and turn upside down to remove excess chocolate. Place truffles one at time into the scoop and roll around until coated with chocolate. Then place the truffle into the cocoa powder. Move the truffle around to coat and leave in the coating for 10 to 15 seconds before removing and placing on a parchment-lined cookie sheet. Repeat until all truffles are coated. Allow truffles to set in a cool, dry place for at least 1 hour; or store in an airtight container in the refrigerator. Truffles are best when served at room temperature.

Del Mar Rendezvous

1555 Camino Del Mar
Del Mar, CA 92014
(858) 755-2669
delmarrendezvous.com
Managing Partner: Daniel Shalom Schreiber
Chef/Partner: Tony Chu Jung Su

Relaxing and casual, the interior design at Del Mar Rendezvous is upscale and appropriate for business meetings and dates, but it's also casual enough for guests to come as they are and enjoy a lunch or dinner with friends and family without feeling stuffy. Located in the heart of Del Mar, Rendezvous is a convenient stroll to many of the shops and galleries, as well as the beach, which is only one block to the west.

"Our restaurant provides the community with a place that they can go to for a great meal and friendly service," says Managing Partner Daniel Schreiber.

Chef and Managing Partner Tony Chu Jung Su creates special dishes from his memories of growing up in Taiwan, as well as modernizing Old World Chinese and Asian recipes with his creativity, attention to presentation, and use of the freshest and highest-quality ingredients available. A menu that includes forty-plus gluten-free items

and forty-plus vegetarian and vegan items enhances the dining experience for guests with dietary restrictions or preferences. In addition, guests can choose from local, sustainable, and organic teas, coffees, beers, and wines. "Our restaurant accommodates all dining needs, especially for guests who are looking for healthy options," Schreiber explains. "Our chicken and ducks are all free-range, cage-free, and natural from a third-generation family-owned and -operated farm in California. The birds are fed a vegetarian diet and are raised and processed naturally—no antibiotics, additives, hormones, or preservatives."

Garlic Wok Baked Prawns is a very unique and authentic dish that can easily be made at home, and the Yu Hsiang Eggplant is a traditional Chinese dish that's well received in the restaurant. These recipes show that even though most of the dishes are American-Chinese, the chefs are also fully capable of cooking dishes that reflect what would be found in the best restaurants in China.

Garlic Wok Baked Prawns

(SERVES 4)

For the prawns:

2 eggs

½ cup all-purpose flour

8 U15 (extra jumbo) prawns, peeled, deveined, and
   butterflied

1 tablespoon cooking oil (corn, vegetable, or olive)

For the sauce:

1 ounce finely chopped green onions or scallions,

1 ounce fresh cilantro, finely chopped

3 ounces or 6 florets broccoli (optional)

3 garlic cloves

½ teaspoon chicken or vegetable bouillon powder

½ cup water

1 tablespoon cooking wine (Shaoxing recommended)

1 teaspoon white vinegar

½ teaspoon sesame oil

1 teaspoon salt

½ teaspoon sugar

To make the prawns: In a large shallow bowl beat the eggs. Place the flour in a separate shallow bowl or on a plate. One at a time, toss the prawns into the flour to coat both sides. Then toss the prawns into the egg to coat both sides. Do this until all the prawns are coated with flour and egg.

Heat a large sauté pan to medium heat. Pour 1 tablespoon cooking oil in the pan. Place the cut side of the prawns face down in the pan. After 2 to 3 minutes, once you see that side has turned light brown, turn the prawns over and heat the other side for another 2 to 3 minutes, until that side is light brown as well. Remove prawns from the pan and place in a strainer to strain the oil from the prawns.

To make the sauce: In a large bowl, mix together all the remaining ingredients. Heat up the pan used to prepare the shrimp to medium heat. Pour the sauce mixture into the pan. Once the sauce is boiling, put the prawns into the pan with the sauce and cook for 1½ to 2 minutes each side. Place prawns and sauce on a serving dish and serve.

Yu Hsiang Eggplant

(SERVES 4)

1 cup plus 2 tablespoons water, divided

1 tablespoon cornstarch

2 cups soybean oil

1 large Japanese eggplant, cut into small cubes

1 garlic clove, chopped

1 tablespoon Szechuan chili paste

1 tablespoon soy sauce

1 tablespoon sugar

1 teaspoon chicken or vegetable bouillon powder

1 cup water

2 teaspoons white vinegar

Mix 2 tablespoons water and cornstarch together and set aside. Pour the soybean oil in a frying pan over high heat. Cook the eggplant in the oil for about 3 to 4 minutes, until it turns a golden color. Strain the eggplant from the oil and remove from the pan, leaving only what oil remains in the pan

(1 to 2 teaspoons) to coat the pan. Reduce the heat to medium and place the chopped garlic into the pan and stir for roughly 10 seconds, until you start to smell the aroma coming from the pan.

Add the Szechuan chili paste to the pan and stir for about 20 seconds, until you start to smell the aroma coming from the pan. Next stir in the soy sauce, sugar, chicken or vegetable powder, and 1 cup water. Wait until the sauce comes to a boil and then place the eggplant back into the pan. Cook and stir for 3 to 4 minutes to ensure that all sides of the eggplant are covered in sauce.

Stir the cornstarch and water mixture into the pan. Once you see that the sauce has coagulated (become sticky/thickened) or after roughly 30 seconds, turn off the heat and mix in the white vinegar. Place on a serving dish and serve.

El Take It Easy

3926 30th Street
San Diego, CA 92104
(619) 291-1859
hubcapsd.com
Proprietor: Jay Porter
Executive Chef: Max Bonacci

Formerly a mainstay in North Park which served new Baja California cuisine, El Take It Easy closed its doors on April 22, 2013. A month later, owner Jay Porter opened a new venture in the same location called, Hubcap, that features a burger menu with eclectic toppings and an interesting array of appetizers.

In 2005 Porter began his career at the Linkery in downtown. It was the first San Diego restaurant to extend a local, farm-to-table approach throughout the menu, including meats, seafood, and drinks. In 2010 Porter opened El Take It Easy in the center of North Park's Restaurant Row with the idea of allowing his patrons to experience local food as something that isn't constrained by the wall that runs

through the middle of the city's metropolis. "We wanted to explore local food without geopolitical considerations, instead focusing on the ingredients and our shared culture in the region," Porter says.

Porter considered his eatery to be a part of the Mexican wine country culinary region that's centered about sixty miles south of downtown San Diego, in the Ensenada and Valle de Guadalupe areas. "We work(ed) almost exclusively with products local to our area, in order to express through food what it means to live in this place at this time. It isn't Mexican food, it's food inspired by what the best Mexican chefs are cooking in our own region."

Porter says it's easy to have a healthy diet when eating in restaurants. "The key is to focus on getting excellent-quality fats in moderation and ordering only foods that contain protein, fruits, and vegetables, not flour or sugar. Stick with grass-fed beef and wild-caught fish and dishes that have good fats, such as real olive oil instead of canola oil or other manufactured fats."

Porter's recipe for Mackerel Wings is easy for the home cook because it doesn't involve any special equipment or hard-to-find ingredients, yet it allows the nonprofessional chef an opportunity to create something different and flavorful.

Mackerel Wings

(SERVES 4)

For the chicken:

20 pastured chicken wings
3 cups chicken stock
Olive oil

For the mackerel sauce:

2 whole sierra mackerel, salted and finely chopped
3 whole limes, juiced
6 cups Shoyu soy sauce (Eden cedar cask-aged
    recommended)
2 cups granulated sugar
1 cup white vinegar
2 cups water
¼ cup Korean chili paste
3 shoots lemongrass
3 cups chicken stock, (leftover from the cooked wings)

To plate:

1 cup crushed pistachios, for garnish
Your favorite dried peppers, cut into slivers, for garnish

To make the chicken: Preheat oven to 350°F. Place chicken wings in a large baking dish and pour chicken stock on top. Bake chicken until cooked through.

To make the mackerel sauce: In a large bowl combine all the mackerel sauce ingredients.

To plate: Coat a large pan with olive oil and warm the chicken wings until just hot (this is to preheat the wings only). Place the wings on a serving platter. Drizzle mackerel sauce over the wings and top with crushed pistachios. Top the wings with slivers of your favorite dried peppers.

FINCH'S BISTRO AND WINE BAR

7644 GIRARD AVENUE
LA JOLLA, CA 92037
(858) 456-4056
FINCHSLAJOLLA.COM
OWNERS: LINDA RAVDEN AND TIANA RAVDEN
EXECUTIVE CHEF: MARIO MEDINA

The Ravden family opened Finch's in March 2010 after realizing that their current space had the potential to become an intimate wine bar and elegant, approachable, romantic, candlelit European-style bistro that showcases an eclectic international gourmet menu. The restaurant is run by the mother–and–daughter-in-law team of Linda and Tiana Ravden, each of whom brings her own unique skills to the table. Today Finch's remains true to its original vision: It has garnered a loyal following among the locals, but it also attracts foodies and music lovers from all over San Diego.

Since the owners have long enjoyed entertaining at home, they brought that same warmth and personal touch to the restaurant. Guests often say that dining at Finch's is like dining in a private home. With an adventurous and ever-changing menu that features a mix of family recipes and unique dishes with an international flair that the Ravdens discovered on their travels, the overall guiding spirit of Finch's is that it's a true gourmet dining experience at casual dining prices. "The Kobe burger is a recipe that everyone will love," says Executive Chef Mario Medina. "It's a definite crowd-pleaser, and we use the highest-quality ingredients to create an American favorite."

Medina says cooking is his passion and, more than anything else, he likes to know that his guests are enjoying his creations. "Working with talented chefs in different cuisines and techniques has opened my eyes to a wide range of both products and cooking styles," he explains. "I have taken the various techniques I have learned under great chefs and have made them my own; they fit my personality and style. I always keep in mind what our guests will enjoy and like the most—not just the cooking but the presentation as well."

Kobe Burgers

(SERVES 4)

2 pounds Kobe ground beef
¼ cup chopped white onions
¼ cup panko bread crumbs
2 tablespoons garlic powder
Pinch salt and pepper
2 tablespoons Worcestershire sauce
¼ cup ketchup
¾ cup olive oil
½ cup bacon, chopped
¼ cup chopped mushrooms
¼ cup sliced white onion
Butter, for buns
4 ciabatta buns or your favorite hamburger buns
½ cup fontina cheese
1 avocado, peeled and sliced

In a large bowl, combine the Kobe beef, chopped white onions, bread crumbs, garlic powder, salt, pepper, Worcestershire sauce, and ketchup. With your hands, form meat into four separate patties. Grill burgers to desired temperature.

In a large frying pan set on medium heat, add olive oil and cook the bacon. Once the bacon is cooked through, add mushrooms and sliced onions and cook until caramelized.

Spread some butter on the inside of the buns and grill for a few minutes. Turn the buns over, add fontina cheese, and allow the cheese to melt. Take buns off the grill and place each on a serving plate. Add a burger patty, some bacon mixture, and sliced avocado to each bun.

FIRST Avenue Bar & Grille

Bristol Hotel
1055 First Avenue
San Diego, CA 92101
(619) 232-6141
FIRSTAVENUEGRILLE.COM
Corporate Executive Chef: Keith A. Lord

Fine dining meets casual date night at this cozy out-of-the-way eatery tucked inside the Bristol Hotel in downtown San Diego. In addition, there's somewhat of a retro feel to the dining room and lounge. "We really whisk you away to another time when you are swaddled in one of our intimate booths," says Corporate Executive Chef Keith A. Lord. "The horse-shoe-shaped bar is super swanky and feels like a 'Bay Area Bourbon Bar.' And, since FIRST is within walking distance to the concert hall and many of the theaters, it is also a very popular pre- and post-show dining spot."

A graduate of the New England Culinary Institute in Essex, Vermont, Chef Lord credits his French-Canadian mother for instigating his lifelong love of cooking, as well as the many chefs and restaurateurs who have inspired him during what he calls his "culinary odyssey." "I love to feed people and make them happy. I'm super creative, artistic, and somewhat crazy with my drive and approach toward new ideas, products, ingredients, and techniques," he says. "But I'm also introverted and somewhat shy. What I may lack as a conversationalist, I can make up for by creating a connection with people through my food, and for me there is no greater joy."

Passionate about his profession, Chef Lord has cooked in many locales, including several states, the islands, Canada, and internationally. "This has had a huge influence on my love of Japanese-farm style, Tunisian, Moroccan, Lebanese, Indian, Northern Californian, and French cooking."

Chef Lord says the Pepper Steak with Arugula Salad and Mashed Potato Puree at FIRST is a "go-to" menu item in the restaurant. The sauce is quite different than the classic au poivre, although the idea of the flavors remain the same. "I've been making my pepper steak this way since the days when I was chef at Linq, an ultra-chic boutique restaurant and lounge in Beverly Hills."

Pepper Steak with Arugula Salad & Mashed Potato Puree

(SERVES 4)

For the steak:

4 (5-ounce) pieces of flat iron steak

For the truffle potato puree:

1 pound Yukon gold potatoes, peeled and cut
8 tablespoons butter
1 cup half-and-half
Truffle oil to taste
Salt and pepper to taste

For the brandy peppercorn sauce:

4 tablespoons shallots
2 tablespoons whole black peppercorns
4 ounces chardonnay
4 bay leaves
½ cup beef stock
½ cup heavy cream
¼ cup brandy

For the arugula salad:

4 cups arugula
4 tablespoons olive oil
2 tablespoons fresh lemon juice
Salt and pepper to taste

To make the steak: Prepare a grill or barbecue to medium-high heat. Cook steaks medium-rare to medium (based on preference).

To make the truffle potato puree: Boil the potatoes until tender. Strain and mash with butter, half-and-half, truffle oil, salt, and pepper. Set aside.

To make the brandy peppercorn sauce: In a large sauté pan over medium heat, sauté the shallots until they become transparent, then add the peppercorns. Add the chardonnay, bay leaves, and beef stock and turn the heat to high. Continue to let the mixture simmer on high heat, stirring frequently, until it reduces by half. Add the heavy cream and brandy and cook until hot. Strain sauce through a sieve and place in a small bowl. Set aside.

To make the arugula salad: In a large bowl toss the arugula with oil and lemon, then season with salt and pepper.

To plate: Mound a quarter of the potatoes in the center of each dinner plate. Place some arugula beside it. Place a piece of steak on top of the potatoes and drizzle sauce on top of the steak and around plate.

FLAVOR DEL MAR

1555 CAMINO DEL MAR
(858) 755-3663
DEL MAR, CA 92014
FLAVORDELMAR.COM
EXECUTIVE CHEF: BRIAN REDZIKOWSKI

With a gorgeous view of the ocean, this unpretentious restaurant in old Del Mar offers a little something for everyone. The ultramodern interior bar and dining room are complemented by a fully enclosed patio with corner fireplace and large windows. It's no wonder this location draws crowds all weekend or at the end of a long business day. Sunsets are especially popular, with the panoramic shoreline vista only a block to the west.

Executive Chef Brian Redzikowski says he loves being a chef because he enjoys working with his crew to lead the progression of food from the soil, to the farmer, to the kitchen, and eventually to the customer. "I'm able to recruit and surround myself with the most talented people. Orchestrating a kitchen crew, building motivation, and being able to bring my colleagues up through the ranks to lead their own kitchens someday is very important to me."

The simplicity of Chef Redzikowski's menu and the best possible ingredients are what keep guests curious about trying new entrees during the changing seasons. "My philosophy has always been to search out the best possible ingredients," he says. "If that's one thousand miles away, I would rather do that than get a mediocre product from my backyard."

Chef Redzikowski offers his recipes for Chicken Coconut Soup and Pickled Potatoes, saying both dishes have been on the menu since he started and are the most popular and well liked by his patrons. "The soup was inspired by my trip to Thailand, although I use a more French-influenced approach to

its execution. I love the balance of sweet, salty, sour, and tart all in one. It gets the taste buds going. The Pickled Potatoes are a very simple yet sophisticated dish based off of great quality ingredients that can be purchased at any store and made into my version of salted chips and vinegar."

CHICKEN COCONUT SOUP

(SERVES 2)

4 cups coconut milk

4 cups chicken stock

4 tablespoons fish sauce

1 lemongrass stalk

2 Kaffir lime leaves

1 tablespoon granulated sugar

Juice of 4 limes

2 tablespoons red curry paste

2 tablespoons minced ginger

½ white onion, peeled and thinly sliced

2 garlic cloves

White or brown rice (optional)

Combine all ingredients except rice in a large saucepan over high heat. Bring mixture to a boil, reduce heat, and simmer for 30 minutes. Remove pan from heat and cover with plastic wrap for 30 minutes. Strain soup through a sieve to remove large pieces. Serve with white or brown rice, if desired.

PICKLED POTATOES

(SERVES 2)

3 cups white vinegar
1 cup granulated sugar
1 cup kosher salt
1 serrano pepper
16 black peppercorns
16 white peppercorns
1 bay leaf
4 cups fingerling potatoes
Canola oil, for frying
Crème fraîche (available at any grocery store)
Handful of fresh chives, finely chopped, for garnish

In a large saucepan, bring vinegar, sugar, salt, pepper, peppercorns, and bay leaf to a boil. Add potatoes. Cook until fork-tender. Remove from heat. Cool at room temperature.

Dry potatoes on paper towels. In a large pot or deep-fryer, heat oil to 350°F. Add the potatoes and fry until the edges are brown. (If desired, potatoes can be pan-fried in oil). Dry potatoes well on paper towels.

Serve potatoes with crème fraîche and chives.

Humphreys Restaurant

Humphreys Half Moon Inn & Suites
2241 Shelter Island Drive
San Diego, CA 92106
(619) 224-3577
HUMPHREYSBYTHEBAY.COM
Executive Chef: Paul Murphy

With stunning views of the San Diego Bay and Executive Chef Paul Murphy's commitment to seasonal ingredients, this hotel restaurant is a cut above the rest. "We use sustainable seafood and local produce as much as we can," says Murphy. "You don't see that often in a hotel restaurant. We even source our water from the most sustainable local water company in the area."

Chef Murphy is self-taught, having learned to cook from working in many different restaurants over the years. He also spent some time in France, where he opened a restaurant. "Humphreys has been around as long as the concert venue located adjacent to the property, and we have evolved with the times," he says. "I'm convinced we have the best view and the most heart of any restaurant in the county."

Chef Murphy says he cooks a selection of menu items using flavors from around the world for his guests as well as for some of the greatest musicians on Earth. "I have the ability to make it happen whatever the request may be. When I walk through the dining room and a guest stops me and says, 'Thank you for that wonderful meal,' I melt. Not to mention that working with legendary music artists each summer during concert season for the last ten years has taught me to be tenacious."

Chef Murphy's recipes for Braised Kurobuta Pork Shank with Ginger Whipped Yams and Macadamia Cake with Warm Coconut Sauce are very approachable. "Neither of these recipes will scare off the general eater—from eating them or trying to prepare them at home," he says.

For cooking healthy meals at home, Chef Murphy says cut out butter and marinate meats and fish with citrus juices and olive oil. Bake items in the oven instead of using the grill. As for eating out, forget the bread and have a small appetizer and share it. Order a seafood entree, skip the starch, and get fruit for dessert. "My favorite snack now is raw cucumber with homemade hummus," he says. "We make a mean sesame hummus at our restaurant."

Braised Kurobuta Pork Shank with Ginger Whipped Yams

(SERVES 6)

For the pork shank:

½ cup all-purpose flour

2 tablespoons onion powder

1 tablespoon paprika

½ teaspoon ground mustard

Kosher salt and freshly ground black pepper to taste

6 (22-ounce) bone-in pork shanks

½ cup extra-virgin olive oil, divided

1 medium onion, chopped

3 jumbo carrots, chopped

3 celery stalks, chopped

4 cloves garlic, chopped

1½ cups white wine

4 cups demi-glace (available at your local grocery store)

2 cups chicken stock

¼ cup fresh thyme

1 bay leaf

For the ginger whipped yams:

3 pounds whole yams, skin on

2 tablespoons butter

1 teaspoon ground ginger

Kosher salt to taste

To make pork shank: In a medium-size mixing bowl, combine the flour, onion powder, paprika, ground mustard, kosher salt, and black pepper. Place the pork shanks in this dry spice rub, coating evenly on all sides.

In a large skillet heat 2 tablespoons olive oil. Add three pork shanks and cook over medium heat, turning shanks periodically until all sides are browned evenly. Repeat the process with the remaining three shanks. Place the browned shanks in a Dutch oven or large baking dish.

Preheat oven to 325°F.

Place a large skillet over high heat and add the onions, carrots, celery, garlic, and remaining olive oil; cook until tender. Add the wine and bring to a boil. Add the demi-glace, chicken stock, thyme, and bay leaf. Return to boiling and then pour this mixture over the shanks in Dutch oven or baking dish. Place the Dutch oven or baking dish in the preheated oven and cook for 2 to 3 hours, until tender.

To make the ginger whipped yams: Preheat oven to 350°F.

Rinse the yams under water and pat dry. Arrange yams on a cookie sheet and bake for approximately 1 hour. Remove from oven and let cool for 20 minutes. Peel off the skins and place yams in a medium-size mixing bowl and mash with a whisk. Add the butter, ginger, and kosher salt and whisk until creamy.

MACADAMIA CAKE WITH WARM COCONUT SAUCE

(SERVES 8)

For the cake:

1 cup finely ground macadamia nuts

1 cup all-purpose flour

1 cup (2 sticks) butter, at room temperature

1 cup granulated sugar

1 teaspoon vanilla extract

1 teaspoon salt

4 eggs

1 tablespoon extra-virgin olive oil

Coconut sauce, for garnish

For the sauce:

¾ cup coconut milk

½ cup heavy cream

½ cup sugar

2 tablespoons cornstarch

For the macadamia nuts:

¼ cup toasted macadamia nuts, finely chopped

Sea salt to taste

To make the cake: In a food processor grind the macadamia nuts with flour; set aside.

In the bowl of a mixer fitted with a paddle, cream the butter and sugar. Add the vanilla and salt. Add the eggs, one at a time, mixing well after each addition.

On low speed, incorporate the nut mixture with the butter mixture until fully combined. Add the olive oil. Cover the batter and refrigerate for 1 hour.

Preheat oven to 350°F. Divide batter into eight large cupcake molds that have been coated with nonstick cooking spray. Bake for 18 to 20 minutes, until golden brown.

To make the sauce: Combine the coconut milk, cream, sugar, and cornstarch in a heavy-gauge saucepan. Cook and stir over medium heat until mixture is almost syrupy. Strain through a fine strainer.

To prepare the macadamia nuts: Preheat oven to 350°F. Place nuts on a baking sheet and sprinkle with sea salt. Toast in the oven for 5 minutes. Remove from oven, rotate, and return to oven until golden brown.

To plate: Place cakes on individual serving plates. Pour sauce over and around cakes and garnish with toasted nuts. Serve immediately.

ISABEL'S CANTINA

966 FELSPAR STREET
SAN DIEGO, CA 92109
(858) 272-8400
ISABELSCANTINA.COM
PROPRIETOR/CHEF: ISABEL CRUZ

Although most of Proprietor and Chef Isabel Cruz's restaurants are similar to each other, they still encompass their own individuality. Isabel's Cantina has a nice neighborhood feel, is big enough to get a table, but small enough to receive good personal service.

Chef Cruz tries to create a healthy cuisine, focusing on authentic home-style Latin food filled with both bold and subtle flavors. Never formally trained in the kitchen, she says she had the good fortune of having some amazing people in her life who introduced her to new foods and flavor combinations. "I truly feel that all my many wonderful culinary influences and experiences show up on each plate we serve," she says. "There's absolutely nothing else I'd rather be doing with my life than continually exploring food."

Offering diverse menus, Chef Cruz believes that one of the most important things she does is seek out as many local and sustainable ingredients as possible. She has a sustainable farm in Sandy, Oregon, where she sources some of her produce, especially for her Portland restaurant. "As we cultivate and expand that farm, we'll be creating house-made sauces and other items that will be used in all of my restaurants," she says. "People should know where their food comes from and how it is produced and handled and what ingredients they are eating. It's critical for the health of this nation."

Chef Cruz's recipes show that wonderful food can be surprisingly simple and approachable. She advises to get creative with her Simple Peanut Sauce and serve it with black beans and rice or alongside a vegetable platter. One of her favorite things to eat, the Panko Shrimp is delicious enjoyed alone or served in a taco with all the fixins. "There are techniques and skills that great chefs possess, but brilliant food can be produced in your own kitchen with ingredients that you already have on hand," she says. "The shrimp is so simple to make, yet it tastes like it could be served in any fine restaurant!"

Simple Peanut Sauce

(MAKES 2½ CUPS)

¼ cup peanut or safflower oil
¼ cup sesame oil
3 garlic cloves, chopped
1 jalapeño, diced
1 tablespoon orange zest
1 tablespoon red pepper chile flakes
1 cup peanut butter
1 cup milk (more for desired consistency)
⅓ cup brown sugar
¼ cup soy sauce

In a small saucepan combine the peanut or safflower oil, sesame oil, garlic, jalapeño, orange zest, and chile flakes. Let simmer over very low heat (to infuse the flavors) for about 4 to 5 minutes, being careful not to let it burn. Remove from heat and allow to cool slightly.

While mixture is still warm, whisk in the peanut butter, milk, brown sugar, and soy sauce. Simmer and stir until combined. Add more milk for desired consistency. Allow mixture to cool, then process in a food processor until smooth.

Panko Shrimp

(SERVES 4)

About 3 cups egg wash (4–5 eggs whisked or
    beaten until creamy)
1 pound panko bread crumbs
2 pounds fresh jumbo shrimp, cleaned, peeled,
    deveined, and butterflied
Kosher salt to taste
Peanut or vegetable oil, for frying (see Note)

Whisk the eggs together in a shallow bowl. Pour the panko bread crumbs in a second shallow bowl. Dredge the shrimp first in the egg wash and then in the panko crumbs, making sure to cover all sides. Season the shrimp with salt and then lay flat in rows on a baking sheet lined with parchment paper.

In a large, heavy frying pan, gradually heat oil to hot, but not smoking hot. Deep-fry the shrimp in small batches, making sure not to overload the pan. Fry shrimp until golden brown, about 2 to 3 minutes, then turn shrimp over and fry on other side. Remove shrimp from oil with a slotted spoon and drain on a baking tray lined with paper towels. Serve warm.

Note: The amount of oil depends on the size of your pan. A good way to gauge this is to fill the pan with oil to 3 inches from the top.

ISOLA PIZZA BAR

1526 INDIA STREET
SAN DIEGO, CA 92101
(619) 255-4230
ISOLAPIZZABAR.COM
OWNER/CHEF: MASSIMO TENINO

Sophisticated and modern, Isola offers warm and friendly service to every guest who walks in the door. Located in a tiny storefront in the heart of San Diego's Little Italy, the menu is a surprise that will leave you craving more for your next visit.

Using a special pizza oven imported from Napoli, Owner and Chef Massimo Tenino focuses on preparing artisan pizzas, using special flour imported from Napoli. "Using water and sea salt, I like to let the dough rise slowly and develop for two days," he says. "In addition to our pizzas, everything on our menu is cooked in our wood-burning oven."

Tenino says his passion for simple fresh food developed as a young boy from his grandmother Isola, who taught him how to cook. Originally from Liguria, a seaside region

of Northern Italy near Genoa, Tenino grew up eating fresh seafood. "Starting in April, when the water was warmer, my older brother and I would go to the seashore to fish for octopus, and when we were lucky enough to catch one, my mom and my nonna [Italian for "grandma"] would prepare it grilled with taggiasche olives, potatoes, lemon, and celery," he says. "My recipe for Grilled Octopus with Kalamata Olives, Fingerling Potatoes, Celery, and Red Wine Vinegar brings back those memories."

Chef Tenino likes to transform raw ingredients into something that makes his guests happy. "I am very creative and hands-on with food, and I believe that some of the best restaurants in Italy are the ones located in small rural towns where the chef buys ingredients from local farmers," he says. "I try to buy locally as much as possible."

Located in Piedmonte, Italy, the Pietro Rinaldi Winery is owned by Tenino's brother, Paolo. Tenino says he's extremely proud to serve his brother's wine at Isola and suggests his Langhe Arnies, a light white wine that pairs perfectly with octopus.

Polipo Grigliato Alla Isola

GRILLED OCTOPUS WITH KALAMATA OLIVES, FINGERLING POTATOES, CELERY & RED WINE VINEGAR

(SERVES 4)

1 cup white wine

Handful parsley stalks

10 peppercorns

5 garlic cloves

2 tablespoons salt

1 octopus (4–5 pounds)

Extra-virgin olive oil to taste

3 stalks celery, thinly sliced

1 lemon, juiced

10 Kalamata olives

7 small fingerling potatoes

3 tablespoons chopped Italian parsley

2 tablespoons red wine vinegar

Salt and pepper to taste

4 cups arugula

Prepare the grill so it is hot.

In large stockpot combine the wine, parsley stalks, peppercorns, garlic cloves, and salt. Add the octopus, cover with water, and cook until tender, about 1 to 2 hours. Checking from time to time, make sure you do not overcook the octopus (it should be tender when pierced with a knife).

Remove the octopus and let it cool. Clean and cut the body and legs into big chunks, sprinkle with olive oil, and grill until lightly charred and caramelized.

In a large mixing bowl, combine celery, lemon juice, olives, potatoes, parsley, and a drizzle of olive oil. Add the grilled octopus, red wine vinegar, salt, and pepper. Mix well, taste, and add more seasoning if needed.

Enjoy at room temperature served on a bed of arugula or by itself.

JIMMY'S FAMOUS AMERICAN TAVERN

4990 NORTH HARBOR DRIVE
SAN DIEGO, CA 92106
(619) 226-2103
J-FAT.COM
OWNER/MANAGING PARTNER: DAVID WILHELM
EXECUTIVE CHEF: JAMES NUNN

While there are numerous "gastropub" concepts open in the San Diego area, Jimmy's Famous American Tavern's unique focus is on regional "American" comfort foods versus the "Euro" food often found in gastropubs.

With a unique location right on the water in the striking Point Loma Marina, guests can take in a beautiful view of the large yacht ships nestled in the harbor. Boasting a comfortable rustic-urban-industrial ambiance, there are three distinct and separate areas inside to enjoy, including an intimate mid-century modern lounge in the front of the restaurant that has sofa and coffee table seating, a main bar room with booths, high tops and flat screen TVs for those want to be in the center of the action, and a large fire pit patio.

Certified as a "green restaurant" by the national Green Restaurant Association, Jimmy's is the only area gastropub with this accreditation, which comes through an extensive applied use of recycled building and decor materials, food composting, drought-resistant landscaping, low-flow water fixtures, recycled menus and paper, and other low-carbon footprint initiatives.

First and foremost Jimmy's sources and offers the highest-quality sustainable and organic food products that are available to them, but within this quest, their priority is always to use local products whenever possible. A restaurant partner in the Long Beach Aquarium's Seafood for the Future program, Jimmy's complies with their established program by using only approved sustainable and properly harvested seafood and shellfish species. Virtually all their protein products

are organically raised and free of hormones. All the coffee, breads, and bakery products come from local vendors. They also serve in-house purified water available still (room temp or chilled) as well as sparkling.

"Comfort food for foodies" is how Executive Chef James Nunn describes his cooking style, where he puts upscale spins on regional American classics. And, since David Wilhelm and Chef Nunn both love shrimp, they felt they had to come up with a warm, and spicy, version as an appetizer on the menu. "We were joking about the scene in the movie *Forrest Gump,* where Bubba goes off on the different ways to prepare shrimp and thought a Southern peel-and-eat version sounded good," says Wilhelm.

Jimmy's is opening their second location in Dana Point in Spring 2013.

Spicy Peel & Eat Shrimp in Beer Broth

(SERVES 2)

For the beer broth:

1 (12 ounce) bottle medium-bodied beer or ale

1½ cups water

1 rib celery, finely chopped

1 carrot, finely chopped

1 small onion, peeled and finely chopped

½ lemon, juiced

1 bay leaf

1 tablespoon Old Bay seasoning

½ teaspoon cracked black pepper

For the shrimp:

6 size 16/20; jumbo shrimp, deveined but not peeled

2 tablespoons butter

1 teaspoon minced garlic

1 teaspoon Old Bay seasoning

1 tablespoon chopped fresh parsley

½ teaspoon cracked black pepper

1 lemon wedge, juiced

2 slices grilled sourdough or Ciabatta bread, buttered and grilled

To make the broth: Combine all ingredients in a large saucepan. Bring to a boil and simmer for 15 minutes. Strain through a fine strainer, cool and refrigerate until ready to use.

To make the shrimp: In a medium sauté pan combine shrimp, ¾ cup beer broth, butter, and garlic. Place over high heat, cover, and bring to a boil for 3 to 4 minutes.

To plate: Divide contents of sauté pan between two serving bowls. Sprinkle with Old Bay seasoning, parsley, pepper, and lemon juice. Place a slice of grilled bread atop the shrimp and serve.

Jsix

616 J Street
San Diego, CA 92101
(619) 531-8744
JSIXRESTAURANT.COM
Executive Chef: Christian Graves

Located in between East Village and the Gaslamp Quarter of downtown San Diego, Jsix is situated adjacent to the Hotel Salomar. Executive Chef Christian Graves is so passionate about bringing fresh food into his kitchen that making regular trips to a farm or farmers' market is never a chore, but rather a labor of love. While visiting local farms, Chef Graves says he gets inspired to pick out his own ingredients because it allows him to get a better understanding of products and hand selections. "I get to see what is coming in and out of season," he says. "I look forward to finding cool ways to use fruits and vegetables at different stages." In addition to managing a small rooftop garden at Jsix, Chef Graves also tends to a huge garden at his own home, providing an opportunity to experiment with new techniques and tricks.

Chef Graves has a hands-on philosophy and believes it is important to buy organic whenever possible. Enter his lively kitchen, and it is obvious that almost everything is created from scratch, including breads, charcuterie, olive oil, and vinegar. Even the table condiments are in-house constructions. With a menu that changes seasonally, Chef Graves's special favorites include all varieties of squash, shelling beans, dark bitter greens, pomegranate seeds, sage, and marjoram. He invites customers to participate

in his "Kitchen Experience," where, on one Sunday a month guests can join him for a morning trip to the Hillcrest Farmers' Market, immediately followed by an interactive afternoon of indulgences at the chef's table.

Taking advantage of the abundant local catch combined with citrus and herbs, Chef Graves's Grilled Whole Sea Bass recipe epitomizes what California Modern Cuisine is all about. Marrying these flavors with a creamy herbed Greek yogurt makes for a decadent meal. Graves also shares a simple and delicious quick pickle recipe that can be used anytime as an accompaniment or healthy snack.

Grilled Whole Sea Bass

(SERVES 6)

For the bass:

1–2 pounds scaled and gutted striped bass (see Note)
Coarse salt and pepper to taste
Extra-virgin olive oil

For the quick pickles:

1 pound Persian cucumbers, cut into coins
    on a mandoline
2 tablespoons apple cider vinegar
½ tablespoon extra-virgin olive oil
1 teaspoon salt

For the grilled limes:

1 lime cut into very thin coins or rings (as thin as you
    can get it and still be intact)
Drizzle of extra-virgin olive oil
Sprinkle of salt

For the spiced yogurt:

1 teaspoon toasted coriander seed, smashed in
    mortar and pestle (or whatever you use to blend
    your spices)
1 cup Greek yogurt

For the herb and citrus salad:

¼ cup picked cilantro sprigs
¼ cup parsley leaves
¼ cup chervil sprigs
¼ cup picked tarragon leaves
Ribbons from 2 lemons, blanched
Ribbons from 2 oranges, blanched
Ribbons from 2 limes, blanched
1 teaspoon sea salt
1 teaspoon extra-virgin olive oil

To make the bass: Prepare the grill to high heat. Season the fish with salt, pepper, and oil. After the grill is hot, start the fish. (This will take the longest amount of time and needs to be done first.) Cook fish on the first side for 4 minutes, until there are nice crass marks and the fish is cooked evenly, then cook another 3 minutes. Turn the fish over, placing it this time on a less hot spot of the grill. After 10 minutes turn the grill off and leave the fish on the grill until you are ready to serve it.

To make the quick pickles: In a bowl, mix all the quick pickle ingredients together and allow to rest until ready to use.

To make the grilled limes: On a small plate season the limes with olive oil and salt. Grill limes alongside the fish for just a few seconds on each side.

To make the spiced yogurt: Toast and crush the coriander seeds and, in a small bowl, mix with yogurt.

To make the herb and citrus salad: In a large bowl mix all the ingredients for the herb and citrus salad.

To plate: Place the fish on a large platter with the pickles, limes, spiced yogurt, and herb and citrus salad dotted all around. Serve with a side of flatbreads and tortillas.

Note: To prepare the fish, turn it so the bottom side is up. With kitchen scissors, cut from the collar down to the tail on one side of the spine and then again on the other side of the spine. This will free the ribs. Using a kitchen knife, cut along both sides of the spine up to the top of the fish. This will cut out all the internal bones. Then cut out the belly flap. Or just eat the fish as is and avoid bones (Chef Graves prefers this option).

KITCHEN 1540

L'AUBERGE DEL MAR
1540 CAMINO DEL MAR
DEL MAR, CA 92014
(858) 793-6460
LAUBERGEDELMAR.COM
EXECUTIVE CHEF: SCOTT THOMAS DOLBEE

Comfortable and casual with an immense energy, Kitchen 1540 has a great reputation for high-end modern cuisine and superb service, complete with an open kitchen where guests get to see the chefs in action. "I think we provide the ultimate culinary flavor adventure," says Chef Scott Thomas Dolbee. "We create cutting-edge dishes to keep the experience alive."

Taught early on by many cooks and chefs, Chef Dolbee says he tends to take a teacher's role in his management style. "It's much like cultivating a garden: You start with the seeds, some good soil, add water, and watch it grow into something incredible. I feel everyone is entitled to a chance at learning something new. I like to see thoughts and ideas turn into reality and then watch it come of age. To me, cooking should be fun and a great learning experience."

Chef Dolbee likes to push the boundaries of overindulgence with great ingredients and flavor combinations. His philosophy is to continually strive for excellence with playful as well as whimsical cutting-edge cuisine focused on flavor profiles. He creates an experience through his craft by using the highest-quality products available in combination with refined and modern techniques. "Play with your food," he says. "To me cooking is the ultimate job, because there are no rules and the possibilities are infinite. I get to play with food all day long, and hopefully I can make many people smile in the process."

Believing that sustainable and local are always going to be key factors in his menu, Chef Dolbee says this is a trend that is here to stay, with the focus on fresh fish and seafood here in San Diego. The recipes for Kumamoto Oyster and Kobe Beef Tartare with Truffle Potato Chips and Seared Rare Ahi Tuna with Smoked Tomato Vinaigrette and Baked Eggplant and Arugula are Chef Dolbee's favorites because he thinks that they have interesting and unique flavor components that you may not find ordinarily. "They are also two of our most popular dishes."

Kumamoto Oyster & Kobe Beef Tartare
with Truffle Potato Chips

(SERVES 4)

For the Kobe beef tartare:

½ cup mayonnaise
1 shallot, chopped
Cayenne pepper to taste
Truffle oil to taste
Worcestershire sauce to taste
Handful of fresh parsley, chopped
Zest and juice of 1 lemon
Salt and pepper to taste
4 ounces Kobe beef, finely chopped

For the truffle potato chips:

2 small Yukon potatoes, sliced thin on a mandoline
Canola oil, for frying
Truffle salt to taste

For the Kumamoto oysters:

8 fresh Kumamoto oysters, shucked

To make the Kobe beef tartare: In a medium-size bowl mix the mayonnaise with the shallots, cayenne pepper, truffle oil, Worcestershire sauce, parsley, lemon zest and juice, salt, and pepper. Toss with the chopped Kobe beef.

To make the truffle potato chips: Fry the potato slices at 300°F in a deep-fryer. Remove and season with truffle salt.

To plate: Spoon some Kobe beef tartare over the shucked oysters and serve. Garnish with potato chips.

Seared Rare Ahi Tuna
with Smoked Tomato Vinaigrette,
Baked Eggplant & Arugula

(SERVES 6)

2 eggplants

1½ cups extra-virgin olive oil, plus some
    extra for drizzling

Salt and freshly ground black pepper to taste

1 onion, peeled and julienned

1 bunch fresh thyme

Balsamic syrup, for drizzling

1 cup alder wood chips

6 large tomatoes, peeled and seeded

½ cup red wine vinegar

1 teaspoon Dijon mustard

1 teaspoon honey

½ cup chopped shallots

¼ cup capers, chopped

½ cup fresh tarragon, chopped

6 (4-ounce) pieces sushi grade tuna, cut into
    ¼-inch slices

6 ounces baby arugula

Slice the eggplant lengthwise into ⅛-inch slices. Drizzle with olive oil and season with salt and pepper. Grill over medium-high heat, turning frequently. Remove from grill and let cool.

Heat a skillet with some olive oil over medium-low heat and sauté the onions until they are brown and caramelized. Remove from heat and let cool.

Preheat oven to 300°F. Layer some of the eggplant slices in a small casserole dish. Then spread a layer of caramelized onions over the eggplant. Sprinkle with fresh thyme and a good drizzle of balsamic syrup. Repeat steps until you have four layers. Cover with aluminum foil and bake for 1½ hours. Let cool, cut into 1-inch squares, and set aside.

Place alder wood chips in a smoker. Place peeled and seeded tomatoes on a wire rack in the smoker and smoke for 10 minutes.

To make the smoked tomato vinaigrette, whisk together the red wine vinegar, mustard, and honey in a medium-size bowl. Slowly whisk in 1½ cups olive oil to create an emulsion. Season to taste with salt and freshly ground black pepper. Dice the smoked tomatoes and place in a mixing bowl. Cover tomatoes with the vinaigrette and add the shallots, capers, and tarragon.

Season the tuna with salt and freshly ground black pepper. Heat a large nonstick sauté pan over medium-low heat. Sear the tuna on one side only about 30 seconds, leaving the top half rare.

Place a spoonful of smoked tomato vinaigrette on the center of each plate and top with seared tuna. Warm the eggplant for 2 minutes in a 350°F oven and arrange on the plate next to the tuna. In a bowl, toss the arugula with some olive oil, salt, and pepper and garnish around the plate.

KITCHEN 4140

4140 MORENA BOULEVARD
SAN DIEGO, CA 92117
(858) 483-4140
KITCHEN4140.COM
OWNER/EXECUTIVE CHEF: KURT METZGER

It all started with Concept Catering by CK (Chef Kurt) in 2000. Chef Kurt established an upscale boutique catering business that was thriving. Several years later he and his wife wanted to expand and offer approachable gourmet food—the Makings of a Mindful Chef!

Kitchen 4140 redefines everything you thought you knew about organic, farm fresh, and sustainable cuisine, focusing on two key points: Use locally sourced ingredients and take all the time needed to create every dish to utter perfection. Founded by Executive Chef Kurt Metzger, the building underwent a complete and thoughtful overhaul before being opened to the public in late 2010.

Off the beaten path, located an easy drive from the busy streets of San Diego, Kitchen 4140 can be found tucked away at the quiet north end of Morena Boulevard. The space itself was designed with reclaimed wood and metal from a local barn, wall tiles from a small remnant shop in Riverside, tables and chairs handpicked in Los Angeles, and a glorious chandelier that Chef Metzger purchased while on a trip to Quebec with his wife. Chef Metzger had a local linen company create the restaurant's strikingly colorful orange napkins and glasses, and every wine glass in the house was handblown in Austria under Chef Metzger's close watch.

Lovingly nicknamed "The Kitchen," this innovative eatery has been serving up a variety of breakfasts, lunches, and brunches since fall 2010. "Fast food is a term that need not be spoken here," says Chef Meztger. "Some fans have been known to fly in from faraway locales just to experience the tasty fare. The freshness that comes alive on the plate is mixed with passion, artistry, and skill. Our Braised Lamb Shank recipe is a perfect example, combining fresh ingredients for an exciting dish. "

The homegrown kitchen, outside the south wall, opens up to The Kitchen's leafy patio seating where guests will find an herb garden reminiscent of the kind they might grow in their own backyards. A variety of greens grace the planter boxes that play a central part to the outside space. "This garden's bounties are the exact herbs used in The Kitchen's own dishes, ensuring the delicate flavors are completely organic and maximally fresh," says Chef Metzger. "We also support other local purveyors."

Braised Lamb Shanks
with Caramelized Onions & Shallots
(SERVES 6)

For the lamb shanks:

4 tablespoons olive oil, divided

1 pound onions, sliced

5 large shallots, sliced (about 1 cup)

2 tablespoons chopped fresh rosemary
   (or 2 teaspoons dried), plus more for garnish

6 (¾- to 1-pound) lamb shanks

Salt and pepper to taste

All-purpose flour, for coating the lamb

2½ cups dry red wine, divided

2½ cups canned beef broth

1½ tablespoons tomato paste

2 bay leaves

For the potato and root vegetable mash:

3 large russet potatoes (about 2½ pounds),
   peeled and cut into 2-inch pieces

3 rutabagas (about 1¾ pounds), peeled,
   halved, and thinly sliced

6 small parsnips (about 14 ounces), peeled
   and cut into 1-inch pieces

3 tablespoons olive oil

Salt and pepper to taste

To make the lamb shanks: Heat 2 tablespoons olive oil in a large heavy Dutch oven over medium-high heat. Add onions and shallots and sauté until brown, about 20 minutes. Mix in the chopped rosemary. Remove from heat.

Sprinkle lamb shanks with salt and pepper and coat with flour. Heat remaining 2 tablespoons olive oil in large heavy skillet over high heat. Working in batches, add lamb shanks to the skillet and cook until brown on both sides, about 10 minutes per batch. Using tongs, transfer lamb shanks to a plate.

Add 1 cup dry red wine to the same skillet and bring to a boil, scraping up any browned bits. Pour into the Dutch oven with the onion mixture. Add remaining 1½ cups red wine, beef broth, tomato paste, and bay leaves to the Dutch oven and bring to a boil, stirring until tomato paste dissolves. Add the lamb shanks, turning to coat with liquid.

Bring mixture to a boil. Reduce heat to low, cover, and simmer about 1½ hours, until lamb is almost tender, turning lamb shanks occasionally. (Lamb shanks can be prepared to this point a day ahead; cover and refrigerate.)

Uncover the Dutch oven, raise the heat, and boil until liquid is reduced to a sauce consistency, stirring and turning lamb shanks occasionally, about 30 minutes. Season with salt and pepper.

To make the potato and root vegetable mash: Bring a large pot of salted water to boil. Add potatoes, rutabagas, and parsnips. Boil until vegetables are tender, about 30 minutes. Drain well.

Return vegetables to their original pot and mash to form a coarse puree. Mix in the olive oil and season with salt and pepper. (Vegetable mash can be prepared 2 hours ahead. Let stand at room temperature. Re-warm over low heat, stirring frequently.) Transfer vegetables to a bowl and serve.

To plate: Spoon potato and root vegetable mash onto plates. Top the vegetables with lamb shanks and sauce. Sprinkle lamb shanks with additional chopped fresh rosemary and serve.

La Valencia Hotel

1132 Prospect Street
(858) 454-0771
La Jolla, CA 92037
lavalencia.com
Executive Chef: Paul McCabe

Rising up above the spectacular La Jolla coastline, the legendary La Valencia Hotel is a stunning building with equally stunning views. Built in 1926, this "Pink Lady" has stood in a class by herself for decades, attracting visitors and locals alike for the world-class location, service, and hospitality that make this destination a must-see. Inspired by luxury resorts lining the Mediterranean Sea, La Valencia has long been a respite for Hollywood stars.

Until recently, at the helm of this iconic hotel's award-winning dining locations, including the signature Whaling Bar & Grill and the Mediterranean Room, was executive chef Paul McCabe. A winner of numerous culinary awards, McCabe is a local celebrity, and is often found judging or cooking at various charity events and competitions.

Proficient in classical French, Mediterranean, Southwestern, and Pacific Rim cuisine, McCabe is also a true believer in the Slow Food Movement, remaining steadfast to

utilizing fresh and local ingredients in his kitchen creations. "Sustainable, local, and organic ingredients are the basis of our cuisine," he says. "We have some of the best produce in the world here in San Diego." Frequenting the local farms and farmers' markets is a regular occurrence for Chef McCabe, where he is often seen talking and laughing with his peers while browsing through fresh produce.

Two perfect examples of McCabe's natural philosophy are his recipes for Wild California Salmon with Preserved Lemon Spaetzle and Sweet and Sour Rhubarb Sauce and his Endive and Frisée Salad with Citrus and Balsamic. "These are very basic, but delicious recipes," he explains. "When we have them on the menu, people always compliment us on the flavor and presentation." Citrus flavors are subtly intertwined through each recipe and pair perfectly for a complete meal. The main course is also flexible enough to substitute salmon for another available local catch, changing the flavors slightly but still complementing the citrus and bitters.

Chef McCabe has moved on to new cooking adventures in Scottsdale, Arizona. Having cooked for some of Hollywood's hottest stars, world figures, and epicureans from around the globe, we were lucky that Chef Paul McCabe graced us with his culinary talents here in San Diego for so many years. Best of luck, Paul. We will miss you!

Endive & Frisée Salad with Citrus & Balsamic

(SERVES 4)

¼ cup balsamic vinegar

2 tablespoons finely sliced shallots

1 tablespoon honey

⅓ cup hazelnut oil

Salt and freshly ground black pepper to taste

3 heads Belgian endive, trimmed and cut crosswise into thin slices

2 heads frisée lettuce, center leaves only, torn into pieces

2 blood oranges or regular oranges, segmented

½ cup hazelnuts, toasted and chopped

Whisk the balsamic vinegar, shallots, and honey in a medium bowl to blend. Gradually whisk in the oil. Season the vinaigrette with salt and pepper.

Toss the endive and frisée in a large bowl with enough vinaigrette to coat. Season with salt and pepper.

Mound the salad onto four plates. Surround with the orange segments. Sprinkle with hazelnuts. Drizzle any remaining vinaigrette around the salads and serve immediately.

Wild California Salmon with Preserved Lemon Spaetzle & Sweet & Sour Rhubarb Sauce

(SERVES 4)

For the spaetzle:

2 cups all-purpose flour
2 tablespoons fennel fronds
3 tablespoons preserved lemon
3 eggs, beaten
1½ cups milk
4 tablespoons butter

For the sauce:

1 quart rhubarb juice
1 ripe pear, cut into small chunks
2 tablespoons champagne vinegar
1 tablespoon granulated sugar

4 (8-ounce) salmon fillets, seasoned with salt
  and pepper to taste.

For serving:

½ fennel bulb, shaved into thin strips, for garnish
1 pomegranate, seeds removed, for garnish

To make the spaetzle: Mix all the ingredients except the butter together in a bowl and allow to rest for 1 to 2 hours.

Bring a large pot of salted water to a boil. Press dough through a spaetzle maker or form the dough by holding a large holed colander over the boiling water and pushing the dough through the holes with a spatula or spoon (this must be done in small batches). Cook spaetzle for 1 to 2 minutes, then shock in an ice bath and drain.

In a large pan sauté the spaetzle in butter until it becomes crisp and browned. Set aside.

To make the sauce: In a saucepan add the rhubarb juice with the pear. Bring to a slow simmer and cook the mixture until it is reduced by half. Remove mixture from heat and place in a blender. Add the vinegar and sugar and process until smooth. Place the sauce in the refrigerator until ready to use.

To make the salmon: Sauté the salmon over medium-high heat until lightly browned. Turn the salmon over and continue to cook until the desired temperature is reached.

To plate: Place about 1 tablespoon sauce in the middle of four dinner plates. Place some spaetzle on the sauce. Add the salmon on top of the spaetzle and finish with shaved fennel and pomegranate seeds.

COURTESY OF LA VALENCIA HOTEL

LEROY'S KITCHEN + LOUNGE

1015 ORANGE AVENUE
CORONADO, CA 92118
(619) 437-6087
LEROYSKITCHENANDLOUNGE.COM
OWNERS: DAVID SPATAFORE AND LEROY MOSSEL
EXECUTIVE CHEF: GREG CHAVEZ

Leroy's Kitchen + Lounge is the first and only farm-to-table restaurant on the island of Coronado.

Owners David Spatafore and Leroy Mossel were ready for a new concept after several years of success with other restaurants on the island. They wanted to take it to the next level, and that meant retiring the Beach-N-Diner to make way for Leroy's Kitchen + Lounge. Executive Chef Greg Chavez joined the team at Leroy's, creating new menus, visiting local farms, planning wine and beer pairing events, and being part of a team that wants to put Leroy's on the map well beyond Coronado.

With sixteen beers on tap, ten of which are local; craft cocktails; and a seasonally driven menu that changes weekly, and sometimes daily based on what inspires Chef Chavez, Leroy's has a welcoming atmosphere that's both casual and comfortable. Musical talent performs in the restaurant weekly and art from local artists that rotates monthly is featured throughout and offered for purchase.

Chef Chavez likes to use sustainable, local, and organic ingredients, saying he wouldn't have it any other way. "I love the power of food and how it brings people together. I love being able to create different dishes and work with local farmers, ranchers, and fishermen," he says. "I enjoy watching my kitchen team grow by helping them develop new techniques and identifying new products. I've worked with chefs who took the time to teach me these things, and now it's my turn to give back."

When Spatafore suggested putting a soup on the brunch menu, Chef Chavez came up with Hangover Soup. "I love any kind of Asian-inspired cuisine, so I combined Indonesian, Japanese, and Vietnamese techniques and ingredients to create the soup," he explains. "It's hearty yet light. If you're hungover, put extra chile in it, if you're not, then don't!"

HANGOVER SOUP

(SERVES 4)

2 limes, cut into wedges
¼ pound bean sprouts
1 small bunch Thai basil
4 quarts vegetable stock
1 stalk lemongrass, sliced
3 Kaffir lime leaves
3 tablespoons ginger, sliced
2 tablespoons sliced garlic
½ bunch cilantro stems
1 star anise
3 cloves
1 medium-size jalapeño, cut lengthwise in half
¼ cup soy sauce
⅛ cup fish sauce
1 tablespoon sesame seed oil
Juice from 1 lime
Salt to taste
1 (14-ounce) package dry rice noodles
1 tablespoon vegetable oil
¾ cups diced sweet potatoes
1 carrot, cut into thin matchsticks
4 ounces white onion, thinly sliced
6 beech mushrooms, thinly sliced
2 ounces sugar snap peas
3 cups Swiss chard, hard packed
2 cups Napa cabbage, thinly chopped
4 tablespoons green onion and 4 tablespoons cilantro, chopped and mixed together

Place lime wedges, bean sprouts, and Thai basil on a plate and set aside.

In a large stockpot combine vegetable stock, lemongrass, Kaffir lime leaves, ginger, garlic, cilantro stems, star anise, cloves, and jalapeño. Bring to a boil. Reduce to a simmer and cook for 30 minutes.

Strain liquid through a fine mesh strainer, discarding the lemongrass, Kaffir lime leaves, ginger, garlic, cilantro stems, star anise, cloves, and jalapeño. Place liquid back into the stockpot. Add soy sauce, fish sauce, sesame oil, and lime juice and season with salt. Return stockpot to the stove and bring to a simmer.

In a separate saucepan, boil 4 quarts water and cook noodles for 3 minutes. Strain noodles and then rinse under ice-cold water until noodles have cooled.

Heat vegetable oil in a large sauté pan over high heat. Add sweet potatoes, carrots, onions, mushrooms, snap peas, Swiss chard, and cabbage and sauté for 3 minutes.

Divide noodles evenly among four bowls. Add an equal amount of vegetables to each bowl. Ladle stock over the noodles and vegetables and garnish with chopped green onion and cilantro mixture. Serve lime wedges, bean sprouts, and Thai basil on a separate plate and add to soup as desired.

Local Habit Organic Food & Craft Beer

3827 5th Avenue
San Diego, CA 92103
(619) 795-4770
mylocalhabit.com
Executive Chef/Owner: Nick Brune

California craft beer and local food are featured at this cozy and comfortable eatery in downtown San Diego, complete with an interior that highlights handcrafted architecture from mostly reclaimed wood products.

Executive Chef and Owner Nick Brune originally opened Local Habit as a pizza and sandwich shop, serving a few small plates here and there. "We asked a few of our regulars, and they agreed that we needed to change the sandwiches to small plates," he says. "Small plates changed to 'fine fare,' and that is what we serve now."

Chef Brune says he's a seafood chef, a fisherman who grew up eating some of the best seafood on the planet in Louisiana. He claims to have created "California Creole" cuisine, combining flavors from both styles into a unique experience. "I also have no problem stepping out of my comfort zone. Food can never be conquered. There is always something new to learn."

Devoted to using sustainable, local, and organic ingredients, Chef Brune shops at the farmers' market three to four days a week and makes everything from scratch. "The only items that are not made in this kitchen are the fusilli, because I don't have an extruder,

and the gluten-free crust, because I'm not a gluten-free facility," he says. "We also change our menu monthly, but keep the same menu annually, which allows our farmers to know exactly what to grow for us, which keeps us seasonal."

The Tahini Chicken Sausage with Sautéed Kale is a good representation of Chef Brune's California Creole cuisine, which is precisely what he likes to serve at Local Habit. "The kale—cooked with spicy vinegar, garlic, and onion—is something we ate back home all the time," he says. "The Tahini Chicken Sausage is the California side. We would use pork back home for sure, and the seasoning would be completely different, using paprika, cayenne, coriander, bay, and allspice."

Tahini Chicken Sausage with Sautéed Kale

(SERVES 8)

For the tahini chicken sausage:

4 tablespoons tahini paste
¼ tablespoon lemon juice
¼ tablespoon salt
½ teaspoon pepper
1 teaspoon oregano
1 teaspoon cumin
1 tablespoon olive oil
½ tablespoon minced garlic
¼ tablespoon mustard powder
1 pound ground chicken
1 tablespoon bread crumbs
1 tablespoon butter, more if needed
   to cook the sausage

For the sautéed kale:

1 bunch fresh kale
½ tablespoon oil
⅛ cup diced onions
½ tablespoon minced garlic
Salt and pepper to taste
White wine vinegar to taste
Serrano chiles to taste

To prepare the tahini chicken sausage: In a large bowl combine the tahini paste, lemon juice, salt, pepper, oregano, cumin, olive oil, garlic, and mustard powder; mix until completely incorporated.

In another large bowl combine the ground chicken and bread crumbs and mix well. Add the tahini paste mixture to the chicken, evenly distribute, and cover and refrigerate overnight or for at least 4 hours.

Form sausage into eight 4-ounce patties. Heat a black iron or stainless steel pan on medium heat and toss in 1 tablespoon butter. Add the sausage patties to the pan (in small batches) and cook until done, about 2½ minutes each side. Remove patties from heat and place on a large platter lined with paper towels. Repeat until all the sausage patties are cooked. The sausage patties can be frozen for up to 2 months or refrigerated for 4 days.

To make the sautéed kale: Wash the kale very well in cold water. Remove the stalk either with a knife or just tear it in half with your hands. Place a large cast iron or stainless steel pan on medium-high heat for 1 minute. Add the oil, followed by the onions. Add the garlic, followed by the kale, and season with salt and pepper. Sauté the kale until it begins to brown (do not move the kale for about 20 seconds, then toss it well with the garlic and the onion). Once the kale has cooked about 20 seconds, add the vinegar and chiles. Steam the kale while tossing it for about 1 minute. The kale is now ready to serve with the sausage patties.

THE MARINE ROOM

2000 SPINDRIFT DRIVE
SAN DIEGO, CA 92037
(858) 459-7222
MARINEROOM.COM
EXECUTIVE CHEF: BERNARD GUILLAS

Boasting elegant dining on the surf, The Marine Room's location, setting, and unique approach to showcasing the local farming community, while combining global flavors and techniques, is unsurpassed.

Opened in 1941, The Marine Room quickly became famous as the pounding surf created dramatic displays for the guests to watch. "Our restaurant's atmosphere is romantic with the waves kissing the windows at high tides, while the sun sets over the Pacific Ocean," says Executive Chef Bernard Guillas. "Guests are not just reserving a table, they're joining a seventy-year tradition. We invite diners to San Diego's premier dining destination to experience how each tide brings something new."

Chef Guillas believes that sustainability is the key to the future growth and

development of our world's oceans, rivers, and lakes. "Understanding its origin is guaranteeing the well-being of our planet," he says. "Searching and sharing information will bring strength and knowledge for generations to come. As chefs and restaurateurs our duty is to be caretakers of our oceans and educators to our customers."

Relying on the bounty of the farmers' markets, fishermen, and ranchers who provide the elements, textures, and flavor profiles that Chef Guillas needs to create his cuisine allows him to share his love and passion for cooking while showcasing his local heritage. "To be a good chef, one has to be a good mentor and a dedicated teacher," he says. "Patience, structure, communication, and understanding the behavior of each ingredient are the keys to a well-balanced and thoughtful cuisine."

Chef Guillas's recipe for Old Vine Zinfandel Braised Colorado Lamb Osso Buco with Root Vegetables and Preserved Fruit Polenta is rustic and warm and tastes of the fall season. He suggests that you ask your butcher for a volcano cut, which is the cutting of the top part of the bone that has very little meat and is easy to cook. "When braising, use a good red wine and make sure that you pour a glass for yourself," he says. "Braising is always done at low temperature to avoid shrinkage and promote tenderness."

Old Vine Zinfandel Braised Colorado Lamb Osso Buco with Root Vegetables & Preserved Fruit Polenta

(SERVES 6)

For the gremolata:

¼ cup minced parsley
1 garlic clove, minced
1 lemon rind, grated

For the old vine zinfandel braised Colorado lamb osso buco:

3 tablespoons grape seed oil
6 (1–1½ pounds) lamb shanks, volcano cut each, if possible
Salt and pepper to taste
2 cups peeled, ½-inch dice carrots
2 cups peeled, ½-inch dice celery roots
1 cup peeled, ½-inch dice parsnips
1 cup peeled pearl onions
6 large tomatoes, coarsely chopped
6 sprigs thyme
3 bay leaves
6 garlic cloves, peeled and crushed
1 bottle old vine zinfandel
2 cups vegetable stock

For the preserved fruit polenta:

4 cups vegetable stock
Pinch saffron
1½ cups cornmeal
½ cup roasted pine nuts
¼ cup diced sun-dried plums
¼ cup sliced sun-dried apricots
¼ cup sun-dried cherries
¼ cup quartered sun-dried figs
½ cup goat cheese
Sea salt and freshly ground black pepper

To plate:

1 tablespoon truffle oil
6 sprigs lemon thyme

To make the gremolata: **Combine all ingredients in a small bowl. Set aside.**

To make the old vine zinfandel lamb osso buco: Preheat oven to 350°F.

Heat oil in a large ovenproof and lidded casserole dish or Dutch oven over high heat until the oil is almost smoking. Season the lamb shanks with salt and pepper, add to the pot, and brown on all sides. Remove the shanks.

Reduce heat to medium and add the carrots, celery, parsnips, and onions. Cook until the vegetables are nicely caramelized, scraping the bottom of the dish, about 5 minutes. Add the tomatoes, thyme, bay leaves, and garlic. Pour in the old vine zinfandel.

Return the shanks to the casserole dish or Dutch oven, cover with vegetable stock, and bring to a boil. Cover and place the dish in the preheated oven. Braise the shanks until fork-tender, about 2 hours.

Remove the shanks and vegetables. Set aside and keep warm. Skim fat from the liquid and place the casserole dish or Dutch oven on the stovetop over medium heat. Reduce liquid by half. Season with salt and pepper. Return the lamb shanks and vegetables to pot with sauce. Sprinkle with gremolata. Place back in the oven for 10 minutes.

To make the preserved fruit polenta: **Place** vegetable stock and saffron in a heavy saucepan over high heat and bring to a boil. Slowly stir in the cornmeal and lower heat to a simmer, stirring constantly for 15 minutes. Polenta should be the consistency of mashed potatoes. Thin with more vegetable stock if necessary. Fold in the pine nuts, fruits, and goat cheese. Stir until cheese is melted. Season to taste with sea salt and freshly ground black pepper. Transfer to a double boiler to keep polenta warm.

To plate each serving: **Place** the osso buco on a warm shallow pasta plate. Scoop the polenta beside the osso buco. Ladle the vegetables and sauce on top of the osso buco. Drizzle with truffle oil. Garnish with a lemon thyme sprig.

Market Restaurant + Bar

3702 Via De La Valle
Del Mar, CA 92014
(858) 523-0007
MARKETDELMAR.COM
Chef/Owner: Carl Schroeder

With a casual contemporary atmosphere mixed with the earth tones, this cozy eatery has a sophisticated wine country feel. Chef and Owner Carl Schroeder purchased Market in 2006 with the support of ten investors. He had already been in the industry for nearly twenty years and finally felt ready to move in a more independent direction. "I knew there was opportunity in the area for a restaurant with a farm-to-table focus in a casual setting," he says. "Today, after many years of hard work and attention to detail, we are now a nationally recognized restaurant that has received many awards and James Beard nominations."

Challenged with local ingredients available on a daily basis and spontaneously creating new dishes, Chef Schroeder has a great eye for detail, a strong focus, and a very distinct point of view on his cuisine. "Sustainability is a major focus in the world right now, and with children of my own, it's definitely important to me to leave as small a footprint as possible," he explains. "Along with this concept I use pesticide-free and local products when available. I believe buying from local farmers and fishermen not only helps the community, it also provides our guests with the highest-quality products."

Constantly making efforts to source the best products available, Chef Schroeder works closely with small farmers and local fishermen. A driving force behind a motivated

crew that strives to invent a new and special cuisine each day, he moves from grower to grower as the seasons change. "Most of the farmers are very specific in what they grow," he says. "Simplicity and seasonal ingredients are two key components to making great healthy meals."

Chef Schroeder's tips for people who are trying to embrace a lifestyle of healthier eating, even when that lifestyle includes eating at restaurants, is to choose dishes that are simple and truly committed to seasonal ingredients. Both of his recipes here showcase great ingredients indigenous to San Diego and use techniques he has learned in his travels to create a spin on international contemporary food.

CABERNET BRAISED BEEF SHORT RIBS & ROASTED TOMATO TART WITH SWEET CORN & CARAMELIZED ONION SAUTÉ

(SERVES 6)

For the short ribs:

2 tablespoons olive oil

18 beef short ribs, deboned

Salt and pepper to taste

2 slices of bacon, chopped

2 yellow onions, peeled and chopped

1 large carrot, chopped

1 rib celery, chopped

2 quarts prepared demi-glace
   (available at most grocery stores)

1 bottle cabernet wine

2 bay leaves

¼ bunch fresh thyme, chopped

¼ bunch fresh parsley, chopped

For the sweet corn and caramelized onion sauté:

3 tablespoons olive oil, divided

2 yellow onions, chopped

1 stick butter, divided

Salt and pepper to taste

8 ears sweet corn, husked and shucked

¼ bunch parsley, chopped

¼ bunch tarragon, chopped

¼ bunch chives, chopped

For the roasted tomato tart:

6 heirloom tomatoes, cut into ¼-inch slices

¼ cup olive oil

12 sprigs thyme

Salt and pepper to taste

12 ounces goat cheese

¼ bunch fresh parsley, chopped

¼ bunch fresh tarragon, chopped

¼ bunch fresh chives, chopped

4 sheets puff pastry

To make the ribs: Preheat the oven to 275°F.

In a large saucepan over high heat, add olive oil. Season ribs with salt and pepper and sear until golden brown on all sides. Add the bacon halfway through the searing process and cook until the fat of the bacon is released.

Remove ribs from the pan and add onions, carrots, and celery. Cook until the onions turn translucent. Add the demi-glace, wine, bay leaves, thyme, parsley and salt and pepper to taste. On a medium simmer, cook the sauce uncovered until it's reduced by half, approximately 20 minutes.

Place ribs inside a large baking dish. Cover ribs with sauce and bake for 4 hours. Remove from oven and place ribs on a large platter. Strain remaining sauce through a fine-mesh sieve and pour into a large saucepan over medium heat. On a medium simmer and uncovered, reduce the sauce to a heavy syrup consistency. Add ribs back to sauce.

To make the sweet corn and caramelized onion sauté: Pour 1 tablespoon oil into a saucepan and heat over medium heat. Add onions and cook until caramelized, approximately 10 minutes. Add half the butter and turn the heat down to medium-low. Cook the onions until translucent and season with salt and pepper.

Pour 2 tablespoons olive oil into a sauté pan over medium heat. Once hot, add the corn. Caramelize the corn lightly and season with salt and pepper. Add the caramelized onions to the corn and toss to mix. Finish with remaining butter and freshly chopped herbs.

To make the roasted tomato tart: Preheat oven to 325°F.

Place tomatoes onto a cookie sheet and drizzle with olive oil. Spread the thyme all around the tomatoes and season with salt and pepper. Bake tomatoes in the oven for 45 minutes to 1 hour. Set aside.

Mix the goat cheese with chopped parsley, tarragon, and chives and season with salt and pepper.

Arrange puff pastry sheets evenly in a 12-inch tart pan and bake until golden brown, about 30 minutes. Allow the tart to cool. Spread goat cheese mixture onto cooked pastry and cover with roasted tomatoes. Divide tart into six servings.

To plate: Place a sixth of the sweet corn and caramelized onion sauté mixture onto the center of six serving plates. Place three ribs directly on top of the sauté mixture. Place one tart segment just off center, slightly to the left of the ribs. Moisten the ribs by placing a spoonful of the braising sauce on top of each rib.

Local White Sea Bass & Sweet Corn Soufflé with Tomatillo Sauce, Shaved Fennel–Arugula Salad & Cherry Tomato Avocado Salsa

(SERVES 8)

For the tomatillo salsa:

1 tablespoon olive oil

1 Spanish onion, diced

2 pasilla peppers, diced

10 garlic cloves, peeled and finely diced

2 pounds tomatillos, diced

1 teaspoon ground cumin

1 teaspoon ground coriander

Lemon juice to taste

Salt and pepper to taste

For the shaved fennel arugula salad:

1 cup arugula

1½ cups shaved fennel

2 tablespoons cilantro, chopped

2 tablespoons chopped green onions

Vinegar to taste

Salt and pepper to taste

For the cherry tomato salsa:

1½ cups cherry tomatoes, halved

2 avocados, peeled, cored, and finely diced

2 tablespoons fresh cilantro, chopped

2 limes, juiced

Salt and pepper to taste

For the sweet corn soufflé béchamel:

1 cup fresh corn (may substitute canned or frozen)

¾ cup milk

1 teaspoon salt

Pinch black pepper

6 tablespoons butter

⅓ cup flour

For the soufflé:

¾ cup fresh corn (may substitute canned or frozen)

¼ cup finely diced red bell pepper

¼ cup finely diced pasilla pepper

1 tablespoon olive oil

Salt and pepper to taste

4 eggs, whites separated from yolks

1 cup pepper jack cheese, cut into medium-size dice

For the sea bass:

8 (6-ounce) portions of white sea bass

Salt and pepper to taste

2 tablespoons canola oil

To make the tomatillo salsa: Add olive oil to a sauté pan, and cook the onions, peppers, and garlic until soft. Add the tomatillos, cumin, and coriander. Over medium heat cook the mixture until thick, approximately 20 minutes. Season with lemon juice, salt, and pepper. Remove from heat and set aside.

To make the shaved fennel arugula salad: In a bowl combine the arugula, fennel, cilantro, and green onions. Season with vinegar, salt, and pepper. Set aside.

To make the cherry tomato salsa: In a bowl combine the tomatoes, avocados, cilantro, lime juice, salt, and pepper. Set aside.

To make the sweet corn soufflé béchamel: In a blender puree the corn, milk, salt, and pepper. Strain mixture through a fine-mesh strainer and reserve.

In a small saucepan melt the butter and then add the flour. Cook on low heat, stirring constantly, for about 3 minutes. Add the corn-milk mixture and whisk until fully incorporated. Bring to a full boil and reduce heat to a low simmer for approximately 5 minutes. Allow béchamel sauce to cool at room temperature.

To make the soufflé: In a large saucepan sauté the corn and peppers in olive oil until soft. Add the sweet corn soufflé béchamel with the egg yolks and whisk together until fully incorporated, then stir in the pepper jack cheese. In a bowl, whisk the egg whites to form stiff peaks, then gently fold into the béchamel mixture.

Preheat oven to 325°F.

Butter and flour eight ramekins and fill each with soufflé mixture. Place ramekins in a baking dish and bake in a water bath (fill the baking dish with water until it reaches halfway up the ramekins) for approximately 30 minutes.

To make the sea bass: Season sea bass with salt and pepper. In a large sauté pan coated with the canola oil, cook the sea bass over medium to low heat for approximately 2½ minutes per side.

To plate: Cover the center of eight serving plates with tomatillo salsa. Place a serving of soufflé on the sauce, just high of center. Place a serving of sea bass in the center of the tomatillo salsa and garnish the top of the fish with cherry tomato salsa. Place the shaved fennel arugula salad so it's spilling off of the fish to the right of the soufflé.

MISTRAL

LOEWS CORONADO BAY RESORT
4000 CORONADO BAY ROAD
CORONADO, CA 92118
(619) 424-4000
LOEWSHOTELS.COM/EN/RESTAURANTS/MISTRAL
EXECUTIVE CHEF: MARK LEIGHTON CHING

Located within the Loews Coronado Bay Resort, a location that provides excellence in dining, entertaining, and lodging, Mistral is a quintessential destination restaurant offering fresh Mediterranean cuisine served in a less pretentious and casual environment.

The atmosphere in the dining room is romantic and bubbly with magnificent views of sunsets across San Diego Bay, with a panorama of downtown San Diego in the distance. Settled within the bay front and marina, you can also ride a gondola through the local canals for a unique occasion.

With more than thirty years of experience at some of the nation's finest four-diamond establishments, including Hyatt Hotels and Resorts in San Francisco, Phoenix, Atlanta, and New Mexico, Executive Chef Mark Leighton Ching has also served as a personal chef for Dennis Hopper and Conference Services Chef at Robert Redford's Sundance Resort in Utah. Most recently, he served as the Executive Chef for Loews Lake Las Vegas Resort in Henderson, Nevada.

COURTESY OF LOEWS CORONADO BAY RESORT

Today, Chef Ching adds a more simplistic approach to Loews Coronado Bay Resort's award-winning culinary operation, taking the best part of traditional Tapas dining, and expanding to more "worldly" offerings. Their new Global Shares tag line is proving that dining can be a very approachable, inviting, engaging, and almost communal experience.

Chef Ching excels at recognizing flavor combinations at the conceptualization stage, keeping in mind the target demographics that frequent the establishment. "Whenever possible, we source local, sustainable, and organic ingredients, and we are also lucky to have our very own herb garden." He says, "Some of our most popular dishes are the Grilled Watermelon Salad, Pork Belly in Asian Steam Buns, Grilled Baby Artichokes, and Cioppino."

When not experimenting in the kitchen, Chef Ching can be found cruising the coast on his motorcycle or rooting for his favorite teams, the San Francisco Giants and the 49ers.

ROMESCO SAUCE

Romesco is a traditional Spanish sauce that has a sweet, spicy, and nutty flavor. It can be used to spice up any dish that needs that extra kick of flavor. Chef Ching says his recipe is very simple and easy to prepare, but packed with flavor and richness. The sauce is especially applicable to almost any protein or vegetable.

(MAKES 1 QUART, SERVES 8–10)

1 medium red bell pepper
1 serrano or jalapeño pepper, finely chopped
1 small yellow onion, finely chopped
3 Roma tomatoes, finely chopped
2 garlic cloves, finely chopped
1 tablespoon extra virgin olive oil
¼ cup of almonds, finely chopped
1 teaspoon sherry vinegar
Salt and pepper, to taste

Roast the bell pepper on an open flame stove top grill or in the oven. Roast until skin is charred and can be peeled off easily. Remove the seeds and finely chop.

In a large bowl, combine peppers, onions, tomatoes, and garlic.

Add olive oil to large sauté pan. When the oil is warm, add the almonds and lightly toast, about 30 seconds. Once the almonds are toasted, add the peppers, onions, tomatoes and garlic. Sauté until all the items are nice and soft, about 3 to 5 minutes.

Remove from heat and place mixture into a food processor and chop for 1 minute. Place in a large bowl and add sherry vinegar and salt and pepper. Serve with lamb, chicken, or your favorite garden vegetables.

Sauce can be cooled and stored in a covered container for up to a week.

COURTESY OF LOEWS CORONADO BAY RESORT

Museum Cafe

Museum of Contemporary Art San Diego
700 Prospect Street
La Jolla, CA 92037
(858) 456-6427
MCASDCAFE.COM
Owner/Executive Chef: Giuseppe Ciuffa

Located within the Museum of Contemporary Art overlooking the Pacific Ocean in beautiful La Jolla, California, the Museum Cafe is a European-inspired bistro that focuses on fresh and seasonal cafe cuisine, boasting a special healthy spin from Owner and Executive Chef Giuseppe Ciuffa.

Growing up in a small town outside of Rome, Italy, Chef Ciuffa believes strongly in cooking, eating, and using sustainable, local, and organic ingredients. He also owns a very successful catering operation, with flexibility to support a small business luncheon to a large special occasion or wedding. He is a perfectionist, and it shows in the quality and consistency of his creations, from simple to elaborate dishes.

Keeping the focus on top-notch quality, Chef Ciuffa says he has high standards when it comes to presentation. "I like to play with colorful ingredients so I can provide the 'wow' factor," he says. "For me it's all about plain and simple flavors combined with passion." His attitude and outlook on life are infectious, as he loves to converse with patrons on subjects ranging from food to art and everything in between. It's quite a treat to enjoy a superior meal, just steps away from one of the more popular museums in the area.

When Chef Ciuffa was a child, meals were always served in the dining room surrounded by family and lively conversation. His recipe for Ribolitta is a perfect example of his simple upbringing. Literally translated as "reboiled," this hearty soup is chock-full of simple vegetables, beans, and chunks of bread. In contrast, his Mexican Shrimp and Grilled Papaya Salad is a perfect example of his passion for utilizing elements from local sources to excite your palate. Best of all, these recipes are flexible enough to allow for substitutions with whatever is available in your area, allowing you to become creative with Chef Ciuffa's approval.

Ribolitta

TUSCAN CABBAGE & BEAN SOUP

(SERVES 8)

5 cups cannellini beans, soaked overnight in water,
   then drained

½ cup extra-virgin olive oil

2 yellow onions, cut into ¼-inch dice

2 leeks, white and light green parts only, thinly sliced

2 carrots, peeled and cut into ¼-inch dice

2 celery ribs, cut into ¼-inch dice

4 Yukon potatoes, peeled and cut into ¼-inch dice

2 garlic cloves, peeled and thinly sliced

3 thyme sprigs

2 rosemary sprigs

1 bay leaf

1 pound black cabbage, roughly chopped

½ pound white cabbage, roughly chopped

2 tablespoons tomato paste

Salt and pepper to taste

Your favorite croutons, for garnish

Parmigiana Reggiano cheese, grated, for garnish

Place cannellini beans in a medium saucepan, add water to cover by 2 inches, and bring to a boil. Lower the heat and let the beans simmer until tender, about 45 minutes.

Meanwhile, in an 8-quart pot heat the olive oil until hot but not smoking. Add the onions, leeks, carrots, celery, potatoes, garlic, thyme, rosemary, and bay leaf and cook, stirring occasionally, until the vegetables begin to soften, about 5 minutes.

Add cabbages and cook until they are softened and wilted, about 5 minutes. Add tomato paste and stir until it is well distributed. Reduce the heat to low and cook for 10 minutes.

Drain the beans and add them to the pot with the vegetable mixture. Add enough water to cover by 2 inches.

Remove small batches of soup and puree in a blender, then return to the pot. Bring pureed soup to a boil, then lower heat and allow to simmer for 45 minutes. Add salt and pepper.

Serve the soup hot in warmed bowls. Garnish with croutons and Parmigiana Reggiano cheese.

Mexican Shrimp & Grilled Papaya Salad

(SERVES 4)

For the papaya:

1 small Mexican papaya
Olive oil, for brushing the papaya
Salt to taste

For the shrimp:

1 teaspoon smoked paprika
1 teaspoon cumin
1 teaspoon garlic powder
1 teaspoon salt
20 raw jumbo shrimp, peeled and washed
1 tablespoon olive oil

For the salad dressing:

¼ cup lemon juice
¼ cup red wine vinegar
1 teaspoon mustard
1 tablespoon honey
2 garlic cloves, peeled
1 cup olive oil
Salt and pepper to taste

For the salad:

1 pound organic baby greens
½ cup feta cheese
½ cup salted and shaved almonds

To make the papaya: Peel and cut the papaya in ¼-inch-thick rings and brush with some olive oil and salt. Grill until grill marks show. Rest papaya after grilling in refrigerator about 10 minutes.

To make the shrimp: In a small bowl, combine paprika, cumin, garlic powder, and salt. Brush shrimp with oil and roll in the spice mixture. Prepare a grill or barbecue to medium-high heat and cook the shrimp on each side until golden brown.

To make the salad dressing: In a blender combine lemon juice, red wine vinegar, mustard, honey, and garlic cloves. Blend, adding the olive oil very slowly, at low speed until all ingredients are incorporated.

To make the salad: Place the organic baby greens in a large salad bowl. Add dressing to taste. Add the papaya, feta cheese, and almonds. Add shrimp all around the top of the salad. Serve and enjoy!

NINE-TEN

910 Prospect Street
La Jolla, CA 92037
(858) 964-5400
nine-ten.com
Executive Chef: Jason Knibb

From curing their own salmon, to the charcuterie, sauces, stocks, and pastas, to making their our own salami, cheeses, ice creams, and sorbets, NINE-TEN is a casually elegant and food-driven restaurant that seems to remain timeless. This is a restaurant where people come for great food and wine, whether wearing a coat and tie or jeans and a button-down shirt. The staff is exceptionally well trained and educated on the food and preparation methods, as well as wine selections and pairings.

Spending a great amount of time working on the line, doing the actual cooking and plating, Executive Chef Jason Knibb is a hands-on chef, with almost every dish that leaves the kitchen having something on it that he actually touched. "There is no pomp and circumstance for me, I just want to cook," he says. "I don't have a culinary degree, and am pretty much a self-taught chef who has spent years practicing and learning from all the great chefs I've had the privilege to work under."

Chef Knibb says his style is to keep the plates simple, fresh, and clean, while still being innovative and elegant. From produce to proteins, he is always on the lookout for the best and freshest products available, developing his menus around the local farmers' harvests and his hydroponic garden conveniently located onsite at the restaurant. "We can use what we need, when we need it, and pick it fresh every single day," he says. "Showcasing the freshness of the product and letting it speak for itself has always been my philosophy."

Popular dishes that are on the menu year-round are the Port Wine Braised Beef Short Ribs and the Jamaican Jerk Pork Belly with Black-Eyed Peas and Garnet Yam Puree, Chef Knibb's signature dish at NINE-TEN. While his cuisine is certainly not representative of the islands, Chef Knibb says that from time to time he likes to add Jamaican-born influences and spices to his cuisine. "The Jerk Pork Belly is a classic Jamaican dish that I have completely modernized," he says. "I think people enjoy it because it has so much personal meaning to me."

Jamaican Jerk Pork Belly with Black-Eyed Peas & Garnet Yam Puree

(SERVES 4)

For the jerk marinade:

3 medium-size yellow onions, chopped

1½ cups finely chopped scallions

6 teaspoons minced fresh thyme

3 teaspoons kosher salt

3 teaspoons brown sugar

3 teaspoons allspice

1½ teaspoons nutmeg

1½ teaspoons cinnamon

3 teaspoons black pepper

3 whole scotch bonnet peppers or habaneros

9 tablespoons soy sauce

3 tablespoons canola oil

3 tablespoons apple cider vinegar

For the jerk pork belly:

1 (5-pound) slab uncured pork belly

Salt and pepper to taste

2 medium yellow onions, diced

3 carrots, peeled and diced

4 stalks celery, diced

1 gallon chicken stock

2 quarts veal stock

For the garnet yam puree:

2 tablespoons olive oil

4 cups peeled and diced yams

Salt

6 cups water

For the black-eyed peas:

1 cup cooked black-eyed peas

1 cup diced and fried plantains

6 baby carrots, braised and halved

1 tablespoon thyme

Salt and pepper to taste

To make the jerk marinade: Place all ingredients in a food processor and puree. The mixture should be slightly chunky and smooth. Makes 1½ quarts marinade.

To make the jerk pork belly: In a large, covered bowl, marinate pork over night with 4 cups jerk marinade. Remove the pork from marinade, scrape off excess marinade, and reserve. Cut pork belly in half and season with salt and pepper.

In a large sauté pan, sear pork on both sides until golden brown. Place the pork into a large roasting pan that is at least 3 inches deep. Add onions, carrots, and celery to the same sauté pan and caramelize. Add remaining jerk marinade and stocks, bring to a boil, and pour over pork.

Preheat oven to 325°F.

Place a piece of parchment paper onto the pork and then cover with foil. Place pork in the oven and cook for 3 to 4 hours, until fork-tender. Remove from oven and let cool to room temperature. Remove the pork from the braising liquid and strain the liquid into a large saucepan. Skim the fat from the liquid, place the pan on medium-high heat, and reduce liquid by half. Remove the pork belly from the liquid and reserve liquid for later. Place the pork belly into the refrigerator and let cool until firm. Once firm,

cut the belly into sixteen 1½ x 1½-inch cubes. Set aside until ready to deep-fry.

When ready, deep-fry three cubes of pork belly in a deep-fryer until golden brown and crispy. Glaze the belly with some of the braising liquid.

To make garnet yam puree: In a medium sauté pan over high heat, add the oil and yams. Sauté for 2 to 3 minutes and add the salt and water. Reduce heat to medium-high and simmer until yams are soft and the liquid is just about dry (add more water if yams are not cooked). Strain yams and place into an ice bath to cool. Once the yams are cool, add to a blender and puree until silky smooth. Season with salt to taste. Set aside.

To make the black-eyed peas: In a large pan sauté the black-eyed peas, plantains, and carrots in the remaining braising liquid. Simmer liquid until it is reduced to a glaze. Season to taste with thyme, salt, and pepper.

Warm the yam puree and, using square serving plates, dollop yam puree off-center of the bottom of the middle of each plate, creating a decorative "swoosh" by swiftly dragging the spoon across the plate to give the dollop puree a little "tail." Place one pork belly cube at the left top of the swoosh, another in the center of the plate, and another at the bottom of the plate. Spoon the black-eyed pea mixture on top of each piece of pork.

Port Wine Braised Beef Short Ribs

(SERVES 6)

3½–4 pounds beef short ribs, boneless if possible
Salt and pepper to taste
1 cup diced onions
1 cup diced carrots
½ cup diced celery
2 garlic cloves
1 bottle red wine
2 cups ruby port wine
½ bunch fresh thyme
1 bay leaf
4 cups veal or chicken stock

Clean short ribs of any excess fat. Season with salt and pepper. In a large sauté pan on medium-high heat, sear the ribs until golden brown on all sides, about 4 minutes. Remove ribs from pan and place in an ovenproof pan.

In the same pan you seared the ribs, sauté the onions, carrots, celery, and garlic on medium heat until golden brown. Add the wines and reduce by half. Add thyme and bay leaf to the wine mixture. Pour mixture over the short ribs and marinate (covered) in the refrigerator for at least 2 to 3 hours or overnight.

Preheat oven to 325°F.

Warm veal or chicken stock in a saucepan and pour over the marinated short ribs. Cover ribs with foil or an ovenproof lid and cook for 3 to 4 hours, or until fork-tender. Remove ribs from the oven and let cool.

Remove the short ribs from the pan, strain the liquid through a fine-mesh strainer and return liquid to the pan over low heat. Skim fat from the top of the liquid and cook on a slow simmer until it is reduced to a sauce-like consistency (sauce should be thick). Return ribs to the pan, glaze, and serve.

Parioli Italian Bistro

647 South Highway 101
Solana Beach, CA 92075
(858) 755-2525
PARIOLIITALIANBISTRO.COM
Chef/Owner: Piero Tarantino

Boasting a modern decor, Parioli is an authentic and casually elegant Italian eatery that caters to the local community by providing organic ingredients and high-quality meals. Chef and owner Piero Tarantino and his brother Antonio opened Parioli Italian Bistro in the summer of 1997 in a small house located directly on Highway 101 in Solana Beach. "Our commitment to this restaurant is to take pride in doing our own cooking, even though we have many employees," says Chef Tarantino. "We are so proud to be a part of this wonderful community, and we continue to be a favorite spot for the locals."

Using local organic products as often as possible, Chef Tarantino has the ability to incorporate local trendy ingredients and still create classic recipes that are true to his Italian heritage.

"Our restaurant reflects the passion we have for food, and the creative part is definitely my drive," he says. "Food is never boring, and numerous, imaginative dishes can be made using the same ingredients."

The recipe for Small Shell Pasta with Tuna and Eggplant is a combination of ingredients that are widely used in Sicily, where Chef Tarantino was born. "The tuna fishing industry has been going on for centuries on the Italian seas," he says. "The first Italian settlers in San Diego continued the same trend they learned back home, enabling me to source fresh tuna on a regular basis. In addition, eggplant, which is an extremely popular ingredient in Sicily, is also used in variety of dishes."

The Swordfish Involtini with Pachino Tomato Salad is a classic Sicilian dish that elegantly displays the use of swordfish, also widely fished in Italian waters. Combined with currants and pine nuts, it lends superlative aromas of citrus and bay leaves. "Our knowledge of Italian cuisine has been passed on from generation to generation," says Piero. "Our food, whether simple or elaborate, is cooking in style for the family at home!"

SMALL SHELL PASTA WITH TUNA & EGGPLANT

(SERVES 4)

3 tablespoons extra-virgin olive oil, plus more for
    coating the pan

4 garlic cloves, finely sliced

2 thick slices fresh Albacore tuna, cut into ½-inch cubes
    (may substitute swordfish or corvina)

1 cup white wine

1 pound cherry tomatoes

Salt and pepper to taste

½ cup chicken stock

1 eggplant, cut into ½-inch cubes

1 pound small shell pasta (substitute any short small
    pasta, like bowtie or rigatoni)

1 teaspoon butter

½ cup fresh mint, finely chopped

Pecorino-Romano cheese, grated, for garnish

In a sauté pan over low heat, add 3 tablespoons olive oil, garlic, and tuna. When the garlic and tuna have cooked for 2 to 3 minutes, add the white wine, tomatoes, salt, pepper, and chicken stock. Simmer until tomatoes get soft. Remove from heat.

In a separate skillet, add enough olive oil to coat the pan and fry the eggplant in small batches over high heat. Place the cooked eggplant on a plate lined with paper towels to absorb some of the frying oil. Season with salt and pepper to taste.

In a large pot of salted boiling water, cook the pasta until al dente. Drain the pasta, reserving some of the water, and place pasta back in the pot. Add the tuna mixture, butter, mint, and eggplant and toss together. If the sauce is too dry, add some of the pasta water.

Plate the pasta in a large serving dish and garnish with cheese. Serve family style!

Swordfish Involtini with Pachino Tomato Salad

(SERVES 4)

For the filling:

1½ tablespoons finely chopped onion

2 tablespoons extra-virgin olive oil

2 cups fresh bread crumbs

2 tablespoons pine nuts

¼ cup currants

¼ cup fresh flat-leaf parsley, finely chopped,
   divided, plus extra for garnish

For the swordfish:

1½ pounds swordfish, cut into 8 (¼-inch-thick)
   slices by your local fishmonger

1 cup ricotta cheese

1 cup fresh bread crumbs

Extra-virgin olive oil

16 (1-inch-thick) onion chunks

16 bay leaves

2 large lemons, cut into 16 wedges

2 oranges, peeled and cut into slices

Juice of ½ lemon

Salt and pepper to taste

8 long wooden skewers

For the salad:

1 pound of Pachino tomatoes (may substitute
   cherry tomatoes)

1 cup buffalo mozzarella or your favorite cheese

1 cup fresh basil leaves, chopped

Salt and pepper to taste

Extra-virgin olive oil, for drizzling

To make the filling: Put the chopped onion and 2 tablespoons olive oil in a skillet at low heat and cook until golden brown. Add 2 cups bread crumbs and stir until the bread crumbs are toasted. Remove from heat and add the pine nuts, currants, and half the parsley. (You want this filling to be soft enough so that when you press it with your hands, it retains its shape and doesn't crumble.)

To make the swordfish: Further flatten the swordfish slices between two pieces of wax paper, pounding with the side of a mallet or heavy cleaver very gently so you don't break through the flesh. Spread some ricotta on the swordfish slices and put some of the bread crumb filling at the lower end of the swordfish steak (about 1 or 1½ tablespoons of filling per slice). Roll the fish over it and close it with a toothpick. Repeat this for all slices of swordfish and set aside.

Coat the swordfish with some extra-virgin olive oil. Place 1 cup bread crumbs on a plate and roll the swordfish in the bread crumbs to coat on all sides. Assemble the swordfish on the skewers starting with 1 piece swordfish in the center and 1 onion chunk, 1 bay leaf, and 1 lemon wedge on opposite ends.

Preheat oven to 375°F.

Cover the bottom of an ovenproof dish with orange slices. Place the swordfish on the top and drizzle with the lemon juice. Bake in the oven until fish is cooked through.

To make the salad: Cut the tomatoes in half and add to a large serving bowl. Add cheese, basil, salt, and pepper. Drizzle with olive oil and serve alongside the swordfish.

THE PRADO AT BALBOA PARK

1549 EL PRADO
SAN DIEGO, CA 92101
(619) 557-9441
COHNRESTAURANTS.COM
OWNERS: THE COHN RESTAURANT GROUP
EXECUTIVE CHEF: JONATHAN HALE

The Prado is winner of numerous local and national awards for its location and cuisine. Strategically positioned in the architecturally stunning House of Hospitality, it is the only full-service restaurant in world-famous Balboa Park. Surrounded by museums, theaters, gardens, and fountains, the Prado is a destination for both tourists and locals. It is a striking combination of lush landscapes, structural designs, and cultural attractions. With multiple choices for dining, including an enclosed terrace, open-air patio, and lively lounge, it's easy to find the right atmosphere for your visit. The restaurant is also a favorite for catering that special occasion or event.

Executive Chef Jonathan Hale brings a unique style and flavor to his dishes, drawing from an eclectic life and career that spans the globe. Born in India and raised in London, Chef Hale was professionally educated at the Culinary Institute of America in New York City. From there he worked at some of the world's finest restaurants in Colorado and Hawaii, finally landing in San Diego in 2001.

Whenever possible, Chef Hale is adamant about supporting local farmers. He enjoys creating new and exciting dishes and watching his guests marvel at the textures and flavors. It is this dedication that has resulted in consistently positive reviews and a well-executed menu throughout the years. "I use classic French techniques and incorporate Asian flavors, which is my passion, as well as a Spanish feel that is reminiscent of the Prado," he says. "I love the diversity. Every day is different and brings a unique and new challenge."

Drawing from his round-the-world culinary exposure, he reveals the secrets to his now-famous Spiced Szechuan Duck Breast with Blackberries, Currants, Farro, Peppercress and Blackberry Gastrique recipe, a long-standing favorite on the menu. The spicy and sweet combination of oriental spices and mixed fruits complements the duck perfectly. "The duck dish is unique because it showcases a variety of flavors and techniques," he explains. "An interesting grain, the farro is not very common in cooking today, and the blackberries offer a ton of flavor."

SPICED SZECHUAN DUCK BREAST WITH BLACKBERRIES, CURRANTS, FARRO, PEPPERCRESS & BLACKBERRY GASTRIQUE

(SERVES 4)

For the blackberry gastrique:

1 tablespoon water
½ cup sugar
½ cup champagne vinegar
1–2 tablespoons blackberry puree

For the starch:

16 ounces farro
¼ onion, diced
2 teaspoons unsalted butter
¼ cup parsley, chopped
¼ cup dried black currants
Salt and pepper to taste

For the duck:

½ cup whole Szechuan peppercorns, ground
    to a powder consistency
4 duck breasts, trimmed and fat side scored
Salt and pepper to taste
Canola oil, for coating the pan

To plate:

½ cup peppercress or micro arugula, finely chopped
4 fresh blackberries, halved

To make the blackberry gastrique: Place water and sugar in a saucepan and heat until sugar dissolves. Stir mixture until golden brown. Gradually add the vinegar; this will cause the mixture to harden. Stir until caramel melts. Add blackberry puree. Boil until mixture reduces to desired consistency, about 3 minutes. Reserve until needed.

To make the starch: Place the farro and onions in a large saucepan. Cover with water. Cook farro on medium heat for 20 to 30 minutes, until tender but still al dente. Add butter, parsley, and currants. Season with salt and pepper.

To make the duck: Preheat oven to 400°F.

Sprinkle Szechuan peppercorn powder on both sides of the duck breasts. Let sit at least 30 minutes and season with salt and pepper. Coat a heavy-bottomed sauté pan with canola oil and set on medium-high heat. Add duck breast to pan (skin side down). Cook until the fat turns golden brown. Turn over and continue cooking until both sides are seared. Place duck in a baking dish and cook in the oven for 8 to 10 minutes. Remove duck when it's firm to the touch or medium rare. Let duck sit 8 to 10 minutes before slicing.

To plate: Place the farro in the center of a serving platter. Slice duck breast and fan pieces onto the farro. Add the blackberry gastrique. Top with peppercress and fresh blackberries.

BALBOA PARK

Balboa Park is a portion of land first dedicated to public recreation in 1835, making it the oldest park in the United States for this purpose. It was designated as a National Historic Landmark in 1977 and is visited by over two million people every year. Spanning twelve hundred acres and situated just northeast of downtown, it is home to sixteen unique museums, as well as a number of theaters and gardens. Of course the most recognizable attraction is the world-famous San Diego Zoo, which is accessible via a multitude of meandering walking paths throughout the park. One major restaurant is located on-site, but there are many additional choices within a short walk or drive. This is also one of the most perfect locations for a picnic, as there are plenty of tree-lined open spaces and benches placed near ponds and reflecting pools.

Quality Social

789 Sixth Avenue
San Diego, CA 92101
(619) 501-7675
QUALITYSOCIAL.COM
Chef de Cuisine: Dustin Beckner

Primarily known as an upscale bar located in the historic Gaslamp Quarter of downtown San Diego, Quality Social offers a quiet atmosphere during the week, with a focus on craft cocktails, wine, and delicious food. On Friday and Saturday nights, however, this unique establishment transforms into a late-night party scene, complete with upbeat music, dancing, strong drinks, and plenty of people-watching opportunities. Their weekend brunch is a hit, featuring interesting twists to classical fare (think benedicts, biscuits, hash, and French toast), to bottomless mimosas and homemade charcuterie and artisanal cheeses.

"Our commitment is to make almost everything from scratch and to give our guests plenty of choices, even down to the condiments. Whether it's a burger, or one of the daily specials or food promotions, the menu changes regularly to entice our guests with something new," says Chef de Cuisine Dustin Beckner. "I strive to make Quality Social a unique option for the downtown dining crowd, and I go above and beyond the current level of most restaurants in the area."

Chef Beckner keeps creative in the kitchen, offering a somewhat whimsical and playful menu while incorporating sustainable, local, and organic ingredients into his dishes. "It just makes me feel better as a chef and a person when I can help to cut down on the environmental impact that the food service industry has put on nature," he says. "My time spent in the outdoors brings this all full circle, as I see the harmful impacts of not following our practices."

The Mexican Chocolate Cake takes the flavor of a rich brownie-like cake to another level with some slight spices of cayenne and cinnamon. The Reuben Croquettes are a great appetizer to share at the beginning of a meal. They are a simple and compact way to get the delicious flavors of a Reuben without having to eat an entire sandwich.

Mexican Chocolate Cake

(SERVES 8)

½ cup butter, more for greasing the pan

½ cup canola oil

¼ cup cocoa powder

1 cup water

2 eggs

½ cup buttermilk

2 teaspoons vanilla extract

2⅓ cups plus 2 teaspoons all-purpose flour, sifted

1 teaspoon baking soda

2 cups granulated sugar

1 teaspoon ground cinnamon

1 teaspoon cayenne pepper

Vanilla ice cream and fresh strawberries, for topping

Heat oven to 350°F.

Grease a 9 x 13-inch glass or metal pan with butter.

In a medium-size saucepan combine butter, oil, cocoa powder, and water. Cook on low heat until butter is melted and all ingredients are incorporated. Remove from heat and allow to cool at room temperature.

In a large bowl beat the eggs with a whisk. Add buttermilk and vanilla and continue mixing with a whisk until all ingredients are incorporated. Add cocoa mixture to egg mixture and whisk some more.

In a separate bowl combine the flour, baking soda, sugar, cinnamon, and cayenne pepper. Gently fold the dry ingredients into the wet ingredients with a rubber spatula, making sure not to overmix. Pour batter into the buttered pan.

Place cake in the oven and cook until toothpick comes out clean, approximately 40 minutes (time will vary with ovens). Let cake cool before removing from pan. After cooling, flip pan over onto a cutting board and cut into nine even portions. Top with vanilla ice cream and fresh strawberries.

Reuben Croquettes

(SERVES 8)

For the béchamel sauce:

1 tablespoon butter

1 tablespoon all-purpose flour

1 cup hot milk

For the croquettes:

1 cup sauerkraut, drained, squeezed, and chopped

1½ cups finely chopped corned beef

1 cup grated Swiss cheese

1 teaspoon Dijon mustard

¼ cup rye bread crumbs

6 eggs

1 cup half-and-half

2 cups all-purpose flour, seasoned with salt
     and pepper to taste

4 cups bread crumbs

10 cups vegetable or canola oil, for frying

1000 Island or ranch dressing, for dipping

To make the béchamel sauce: Melt the butter in a small saucepan over low heat and mix in the flour to make a roux, cooking for 2 minutes. Add hot milk and whisk until all clumps disappear. Let the sauce cook on low for 20 minutes, stirring regularly. The sauce will become thick. Remove from heat and cool to room temperature.

To make the croquettes: In a large bowl combine béchamel sauce, sauerkraut, corned beef, Swiss cheese, mustard, and rye bread crumbs. Roll into golf ball–size balls. Chill in refrigerator for 1 hour, until firm.

In a large shallow bowl whisk eggs and half-and-half to make an egg wash. Place the seasoned flour in another large shallow bowl. Place the bread crumbs in a third large shallow bowl. Roll one ball at a time, first in flour, then in egg wash, then in bread crumbs. Bread all the croquettes before cooking.

Pour the vegetable or canola oil into a deep-fryer and heat to 350°F. Fry the croquettes in oil until golden brown. Carefully remove croquettes from oil and drain on a large platter lined with paper towels. Serve with 1000 Island or ranch dressing.

Sabuku Sushi

3027 Adams Avenue
San Diego, CA 92116
(619) 281-9700
SABUKUSUSHI.COM
Proprietor/Chef: Bob Pasela

Located in the heart of uptown San Diego, Sabuku Sushi is modern and chic but without the pretentiousness of a high-end restaurant. This upscale eatery is all about the finest and freshest fish and other main ingredients. Nothing is premade or precooked, and guests are given the freedom to substitute, change, or alter anything they'd like to their suit their tastes. Their sushi bar is well-known throughout the county as one of the best.

"In an area where the mix of San Diegans could not be more diverse, I want my restaurant to be welcoming to all, whether a guest rides up tattooed on a Harley or is dressed for a play at the Old Globe Theater and looking for a fine dinner," says proprietor and chef Bob Pasela. "No one should ever feel uncomfortable here."

Chef Pasela believes in striking a balance by using sustainable farm-raised fish, such as salmon, where it makes sense and protects the species, and wild fish, such as tuna, where he says current quantities are not considered endangered. "We use one of San Diego's largest wholesale suppliers and are given access to the freshest and highest-quality fruits and vegetables," he says. "If ever the ingredients arrive not at their peak of ripeness, we're able to send them back."

Chef Pasela likes to take a bunch of ingredients and turn them into a wonderful creation right in front of the guests seated at the bar. One of his most popular rolls is the Red Dragon Roll, which highlights the bright flavors of high-end tuna. "Watching the unsolicited responses when our guest are handed their rolls and seeing their eyes grow wide with excitement never gets old," he says. "Overhearing statements like 'That was amazing!' or 'This place is the best!' is always greatly and humbly appreciated."

RED DRAGON ROLL
(SERVES 2)

1 cup crabmeat, finely diced or minced

2 tablespoons mayonnaise

Sriracha to taste

1–2 tablespoons mirin

2 stalks asparagus

1 (8 x 8½-inch sheet) nori

1 cup cooked white rice

4 thin slices sushi-grade tuna

1 avocado, peeled, seeded, and cut into thin slices

Ponzu sauce, for drizzling (available at grocery stores and Asian markets)

Black sesame seeds

In a bowl combine crab, mayonnaise, sriracha, and mirin. Set aside.

Fill a small skillet with water deep enough to soak a few pieces of asparagus. Bring water to a light boil and blanch asparagus until bright green, about 1 minute. Remove asparagus and set aside.

Place the Nori sheet facing you lengthwise across the table. Form the rice into a log along the length of the sheet. Place the asparagus on top of the rice and add the spicy crab mixture. Close the roll by rolling the nori sheet lengthwise from one side over to the other. Compress and shape the roll with your hands.

Place tuna slices across the roll at a slight angle, leaving a small gap between each tuna slice. Take thin slices of avocado and place one in each gap. Cut the roll into slices.

Place the slices on a serving plate. Drizzle ponzu sauce along the top of the roll, letting it drip down to the plate. Sprinkle with black sesame seeds.

SBICCA DEL MAR

215 15TH STREET
DEL MAR, CA 92014
(858) 481-1001
SBICCADELMAR.COM
OWNER: DAN SBICCA

Sbicca is the perfect gathering place for locals in a predominantly tourist-centric
area of north San Diego. Owner Dan Sbicca says he opened his bistro in 1998 as a
"neighborhood restaurant." Leaving his life as a stockbroker, he wanted to establish
a bistro that felt like an expansion of his living room, with a location that was not only
convenient, but attractive and inviting. "I look back to our first days and see how far we've
come, yet how much we have stayed the same."

Just a few blocks from the beach, guests can experience casual and fine dining
coupled with professional service in a friendly and unpretentious atmosphere. "I always
enjoy listening to the hum and clatter of a full restaurant and all the happy voices," he

says. "Sometimes I see people joining other tables
for food and conversation. Of course the ocean
views don't hurt either." The deck, which has a
stunning view of the ocean, is a perfect location
for a casual lunch, romantic dinner, or a private
party with room for fifty guests. A private and
intimate wine room is also available.

Sbicca adjusts his menu often, offering
specials based on what is fresh and available, as
well as what his guests want to eat. "I listen to my
clientele. Sbicca was built for them not me," he
says. "I am most satisfied when guests tell me how
much they enjoy my restaurant."

Sbicca believes in using flavorful ingredients
that are healthy and excite the palate. His recipe
for Pan Roasted Halibut with Baby Zucchini,
Roasted Corn, and Shitake Hash and Puree of
Cilantro and Parsley is a good example of what
bright and clean ingredients the local farms and
markets of San Diego have to offer. "It's a light
and flavorful dish that our health-conscious
neighborhood wants," he says. "And if you eat a
little too much of it, it won't hurt you!"

Pan Roasted Halibut with Baby Zucchini, Roasted Corn & Shitake Hash & Puree of Cilantro & Parsley

(SERVES 2)

For the puree of cilantro and parsley:

½ bunch cilantro
½ bunch parsley
2 teaspoons Dijon mustard
2 limes, juiced
1 tablespoon water
1 tablespoon olive oil
Salt and pepper to taste

For the halibut:

2 (8-ounce) portions halibut
Salt and pepper to taste
4 teaspoons butter

For the hash:

1 teaspoon butter
1 tablespoon olive oil
4 shitake mushrooms, stems removed and julienned
2 corn cobs, kernels removed
6 baby zucchini, split lengthwise
2 tablespoons white wine

To plate:

6 cherry tomatoes, halved

To make the puree of cilantro and parsley: In a blender combine the cilantro, parsley, mustard, lime juice, and water. Puree and slowly add the olive oil. Season with salt and pepper.

To make the halibut: Season the halibut with salt and pepper. In a medium pan set on high heat, add 2 teaspoons butter and then add the halibut. Keep the heat between medium and

high and spoon 2 teaspoons butter over the fish as it cooks. If the butter starts to darken, lower the heat slightly and add another pat of butter. Once the fish is halfway cooked, flip and continue spooning the butter over the fish until the fish is firm. Remove from heat and set aside.

To make the hash: In a medium to hot pan add butter and olive oil to coat the pan. Add mushrooms and corn and sauté until light golden brown. Add the zucchini and deglaze by adding the white wine to the pan to pick up any flavorful bits. Cook until the zucchini is crisp but tender.

To plate: Spoon half of the hash mixture onto two serving plates, then lay half the zucchini pieces across the top. Place halibut on top of the zucchini. Garnish with cherry tomatoes. Spoon a little bit of the puree onto the fish and a little bit around the plate.

Sea Rocket Bistro

3382 30th Street
San Diego, CA 92104
(619) 255-7049
SEAROCKETBISTRO.COM
Executive Chef: Tommy Fraioli

Tommy Fraioli started his first kitchen job in a small cafe in his hometown of Modesto, California, when he was nineteen years old. Since then he's worked in various different restaurants where he's made it his goal to learn everything as quickly as possible, becoming fast and efficient at everything he does. Within a year of joining Sea Rocket Bistro, Fraioli was promoted to executive chef.

Chef Fraioli likes to spend his time building his kitchen team, offering them all of the knowledge he's gained over the years. "I feel that working the line, and getting the food out quickly and with consistent flavors each time, is one of my strongest talents in the kitchen," he says. "I like being able to get as creative as possible, trying new things and being where all the action is."

With a seasonal menu that's constantly changing, Chef Fraioli is committed to incorporating local, regional, and organic ingredients into all of his dishes. This includes sustainably harvested seafood, pastured meats, vegetarian and vegan options, local craft beer, and California wines. "Not only do I favor freshness and variety, it's also important for me to know where my food is coming from," he says. "Plus, there is such a wide variety of items to choose from." The Sea Rocket website includes a comprehensive list of local sources for nearly every item on the menu, providing an educational view of the local bounty.

Located in the eclectic and hip neighborhood of North Park, Sea Rocket is a comfortable and mellow farm-to-table restaurant that is a favorite destination for foodies. The fare is simple in form, sometimes referred to as "peasant food," but bold in flavors and presentation. Their recipe for Fisherman's Stew is a perfect example of this style, with an assortment of seafood and vegetables in a steamy broth that is easy to prepare and take pleasure in.

FISHERMAN'S STEW

(SERVES 6)

1½ cups diced onions

10 garlic cloves, diced

2 tablespoons butter

2 quarts tomatoes, drained and diced

½ cup paprika

1 tablespoon cayenne

1 tablespoon salt

1 tablespoon pepper

6 cups water

½ pound raw bacon, diced

1 pound mussels, cleaned

2 pounds clams, washed

½ cup diced shallots

1 tablespoon chopped fresh parsley

1 tablespoon chopped fresh thyme

1 tablespoon chopped fresh chives

½ cup white wine

Red pepper or chile flakes, to taste
(optional)

½ pound medium-size shrimp, peeled

Butter to taste

Your favorite bread, for dipping

In a large pan over medium heat, sauté onions and garlic in butter until soft. Add tomatoes, paprika, cayenne, salt, and pepper and add water to cover. Bring to a boil and reduce to a simmer until tomatoes are soft, about 15 to 20 minutes. Strain vegetables from the liquid and place in a blender. Puree with just enough of the liquid to the consistency of a thin soup.

To assemble the stew, cook the bacon in a large sauté pan. Add the mussels, clams, shallots, parsley, thyme, and chives. Add the wine, tomato puree, and chile flakes. Cover the pan and simmer until the shellfish open up. Add the shrimp and some butter and cover until the shrimp is cooked. When everything is cooked, the stew is ready. Serve with your favorite bread.

STONE BREWING WORLD BISTRO AND GARDENS

1999 CITRACADO PARKWAY
ESCONDIDO, CA 92029
(760) 294-7866
STONEBREW.COM
CHIEF CULINARY PHILOSOPHER: ALEX CARBALLO

Best described as "industrial-becoming-organic," Stone Brewing World Bistro and Garden's award-winning architecture embodies an affinity for melding organic features of wood, stone, plant life, water, and fresh air with industrial elements of metal, concrete, and glass. Begun as a small microbrewery in 1996, Stone has become one of the most easily recognized, multi–award-winning breweries in the United States and now distributes their products both nationally and internationally.

Experience a beautiful open-air patio, one-acre organic beer garden, and an expansive craft beer restaurant that offers eclectic dishes focused on fresh and all-natural world-inspired cuisine, offering guests trouble-free dining options they can feel good about. "We buy from other local farmers within 150 miles of our restaurant," says Chief Culinary Philosopher Alex Carballo. "We don't just 'like,' we love sustainable and organic ingredients and make it our first priority to support local sources."

Carballo prides himself on being extremely organized, which allows him to be successful in a competitive field. "I love working with food and being able to embrace my creativity in the kitchen while working with great people," he says. "What gives me the most satisfaction is seeing the smiles on our customer's faces. Without them, I would just be a home cook."

When it comes to cooking healthy meals at home, Carballo advises not to cook with saturated fats, saying that making this small change can make a big difference. One of his favorite greens, arugula, is a lettuce grown on property at Stone Farms, and arugula salads are featured on the menu regularly. Another food staple that Carballo adores, even when he goes out to eat, is the Bahn Mi, or Vietnamese Meatball Sandwich. "It's sweet, spicy, and savory, along with the crunch of the French baguette," Carballo says. "What more can someone ask for in a sandwich?" Carballo shares his special recipe for this staple on the menu, which also offers plenty of excellent beer-pairing choices.

MICROBREWERY BOOM

A microbrewery is quite simply a small-scale, independent producer that uses traditional techniques to create an incredibly diverse spectrum of quality beer. With nearly forty brewers and counting, San Diego has become one of the fastest-growing hubs, receiving national attention at some of the most well-known competitions around the world. One catalyst for this local movement is the camaraderie and community prevalent among many of the brewmasters. Sharing their experiments and successes has helped the region grow rapidly, while keeping a competitive spirit geared toward friendly and positive feedback. This environment has produced some of the highest-rated creations, with many more expected as time progresses. Just stop by any of the crowded neighborhood brewpubs in the area and marvel at the selection of tap and bottled local products. From light ales to Belgians to dark stouts, there's something pleasing for every palette.

Bahn Mi—Vietnamese Meatball Sandwich

(MAKES 4 SANDWICHES)

For the bahn mi meatballs:

1 pound ground buffalo (may substitute any
     ground meat/poultry of your choice)
⅓ cup panko bread crumbs
2 tablespoons finely diced red onion
½ bunch green onions, finely diced
1 tablespoon chopped garlic
1 tablespoon Thai fish sauce, or Nam Pla
     (available at Asian markets)
2 tablespoons sesame oil
2 tablespoons Sriracha hot sauce
     (available at Asian markets)
2 tablespoons sugar
1 tablespoon soy sauce
1 tablespoon minced fresh basil
2 tablespoons fresh cilantro, chopped
Kosher salt and black pepper to taste
1 tablespoon sesame oil

For the pickled vegetables:

½ cup rice wine vinegar
½ cup mirin
½ cup water
1 cup thinly sliced radishes
1 cup julienned carrots
¼ cup jalapeño pepper, seeded and thinly sliced

For the sambal oelek mayonnaise:

2 cups mayonnaise
¼ cup roasted and minced garlic
½ bunch green onion, chopped
¼ cup sambal oelek chili paste
     (available at Asian markets)

For assembling the sandwiches:

4 (10-inch) baguettes or French rolls, cut lengthwise

To make the bahn mi meatballs: In a large bowl, combine all ingredients except sesame oil and mix together well. Shape mixture into golf-ball-size meatballs and place on a baking sheet. (This can be done a day ahead and held in the refrigerator until ready to cook, if desired.)

To cook the meatballs, heat sesame oil in a large pan over medium-high heat. Add half of the meatballs (don't overcrowd the pan) and sauté until brown and cooked through, turning often and lowering the heat if they seem to be browning too fast. They should cook for about 15 minutes. Repeat with remaining half of meatballs, keeping the first batch warm in the oven (300°F).

If desired, meatballs may be cooked ahead and reheated before assembly, using a skillet over medium heat and a mixture of 2 tablespoons soy sauce and 2 tablespoons sesame oil to sauté.

To make the pickled vegetables: Bring vinegar, mirin, and water to a boil in a saucepan. Combine the radishes, carrots, and jalapeño in a bowl and pour the vinegar mixture over the vegetables. Allow to cool, then refrigerate until needed.

To prepare the sambal oelek mayonnaise: In a large bowl combine all the ingredients. Refrigerate until needed.

To assemble the sandwiches: Slice baguettes or rolls in half lengthwise and pull some of the bread out of each half, leaving a ½-inch shell. Spread both sides of roll with approximately 1 tablespoon mayonnaise (extra will keep in the refrigerator). Place 4 meatballs on each roll's bottom half. Top meatballs with well-drained pickled vegetables (approximately ¼ cup per sandwich; extra will keep in the refrigerator for 7 to 10 days). Press on the roll's top half.

TABLE 926

926 TURQUOISE STREET
SAN DIEGO, CA 92109
(858) 539-0926
TABLE926.COM
OWNER/EXECUTIVE CHEF: MATTHEW RICHMAN

Table 926 merges the upscale side of dining out with a casual and unpretentious atmosphere. Tucked in a nearly hidden spot away from the street, this quaint little bistro provides a convenient respite from the daily grind. It's the perfect combination of characteristics for their location that borders two drastically different beach communities: La Jolla and Pacific Beach. What differentiates Table 926 from other restaurants in the community of North Pacific Beach is their commitment to using organic, sustainable produce and proteins. In addition, they pride themselves on offering four to six daily specials, while maintaining a regular menu that is seasonally driven.

A San Diego native, Owner and Executive Chef Matthew Richman has spent much of his career on his home turf after studying and working in other areas of the United States. "We feel that it's important to use ingredients while they are at the height of their season," he says. "It's vital to offer recipes that can be created at alternate times of the year."

Table 926 has an innate ability to take and analyze fresh ingredients, then match flavor components and prepare them in a straightforward way. "We use sustainable, local, and organic ingredients as much as possible, often going out of our way to ensure this happens," says Chef Richman. "We're also fans of Southern California's increasingly popular local farms, which are often the source of our produce."

For starters, or a smaller bite, many guests like to order the Duck Confit "Carnitas" Tacos, served on corn tortillas with pickled red onion and queso fresco under tomatillo-avocado and smoked chile salsas. In addition, diners can't seem to get enough of the Glazed Pork Cheeks served on creamy polenta with Suzie's Farms braising greens, under a guajillo-tamarind glaze or the extremely popular crowd-pleasing Braised Lamb Shank with Mushroom Risotto, the perfect fall and winter comfort food concoction.

BRAISED LAMB SHANK WITH MUSHROOM RISOTTO
(SERVES 4)

4 lamb shanks

Sea salt and pepper to taste

Olive oil, for frying

2 large yellow onions, chopped into medium-size dice

3 carrots, chopped into medium-size dice

1 head celery, leaves removed and chopped into medium-size dice

8 garlic cloves, finely chopped

2 shallots, 1 chopped into medium-size dice and 1 finely diced

½ bottle red wine

1 bay leaf

¼ bunch parsley

5 sprigs thyme

4 quarts veal or beef stock

½ ounce dried mushrooms

1 cup arborio rice

½ cup white wine, divided

½ cup mushrooms, finely chopped

½ cup mascarpone cheese

Your favorite fresh herbs, finely chopped, for garnish (optional)

Lemon zest, for garnish (optional)

Preheat oven to 325°F.

Season lamb shanks well with salt and pepper. Heat a Dutch oven or braising pan on medium heat and sear lamb shanks in olive oil on each side until a nice brown crust forms without any burning (about 4 to 5 minutes on each side). Remove shanks from the pan.

Remove three-quarters of the fat from the pan and return to heat. Add onions, carrots, celery, garlic, and chopped shallots to pan and sauté until caramelized. Deglaze pan with red wine and add bay leaf, parsley, and thyme. Simmer for 6 to 7 minutes before adding stock and shanks. Bring to a boil, cover, and place in preheated oven for 3 to 4 hours, until meat is starting to fall of the bone.

About 45 minutes before serving, place dried mushrooms in 2 to 3 quarts very hot water and let steep for 20 minutes. In a sauté pan over medium heat, sweat the finely diced shallots for 2 to 3 minutes, but do not allow them to brown. Add rice and continue to cook for 2 to 3 minutes. Deglaze pan with white wine and let simmer for 2 to 3 minutes, until almost dry.

Table 926   173

Remove mushrooms from water (reserving the mushroom water/stock) and chop into small dice. While stirring rice, add a couple ladles of mushroom water/stock. Being sure to stir constantly, ladle more mushroom water/stock when the rice mixture is almost dry and not sticking to pan. Continue this process for 12 to 15 minutes, until the rice is to desired texture. Add all the mushrooms and mascarpone cheese and season with salt and pepper. You can add more mushroom water/stock to the risotto until you get the desired texture.

Remove the shanks from the Dutch oven, then place the Dutch oven on stovetop. On a slow simmer, reduce the sauce until it reaches the desired thickness. Spoon risotto onto serving plates, place a shank on top, and ladle shank sauce on top. Garnish with chopped fresh herbs or a little lemon zest.

Tender Greens

2400 Historic Decatur Road
San Diego, CA 92106
(619) 226-6254
TENDERGREENSFOOD.COM
Executive Chef: Pete Balistreri

Casual, comfortable, clean, and lively, Tender Greens is a great place to be a regular diner.

"Some of our good friends have really great restaurants in our area, but mostly our team tries to focus on doing the best we can in our store every day," says Executive Chef Pete Balistreri. "We don't spend much time thinking or comparing to other restaurants. We have too much fun working together as a team and trying to improve our own shop to spend any thought on other places."

Chef Balistreri personally enjoys teaching others to improve, and sharing his knowledge is something he's passionate about. Not only does he pride himself on leading a talented team, he has a ceaseless drive toward novelty, especially with the house-cured salumis and use of sustainable, local, and organic ingredients. "Using natural ingredients is like breathing to us. We do it without even thinking about it. It's part of our existence. It's what we are," he says.

"Our Point Loma store started out doing about one hundred covers a day. Now we do that in an hour or so. We have come a long way, and it's due to the great team we have working here together and the amazing support of our community."

Considered a "fast-casual organic restaurant," Tender Greens has expanded to nine locations in the Southern California region, with plenty of tasteful and nutritious meals available for immediate consumption or take home. They have also developed a very successful catering business, with menus perfect for small dinner parties and backyard barbecues, to large and elaborate celebrations.

The Flat Iron Steak Sandwich with Grilled Summer Vegetables served on ciabatta bread is very popular with the guests at Tender Greens. With the influence of roasted red peppers and a splash of good red wine vinegar and olive oil, make sure you have plenty of time to savor each and every bite.

FLAT IRON STEAK SANDWICH
WITH GRILLED SUMMER VEGETABLES

(SERVES 4)

For the marinade:

1 pound flat iron steak
5 garlic cloves
½ bunch chopped parsley
½ cup olive oil
1 teaspoon red pepper flakes

For the aioli:

2 large egg yolks
1 tablespoon Dijon mustard
½ teaspoon chopped garlic
¼ cup lemon juice
Splash of red wine vinegar
½ cup extra-virgin olive oil, more for drizzling

For the roasted red peppers:

2 red peppers
Red wine vinegar
Extra-virgin olive oil

For the grilled summer vegetables:

Summer vegetables of your choice,
   enough for 4 sandwiches
Salt and pepper to taste
Extra-virgin olive oil, for drizzling

To assemble the sandwiches:

8 slices your favorite sandwich bread

To make the marinade: In a large bowl, combine steak with garlic, parsley, olive oil, and chili flakes. Cover bowl and allow steak to marinate in the refrigerator for 2 to 4 hours.

To make the aioli: Place all ingredients except the olive oil in a food processor or blender and mix together slowly. Slowly drizzle in the olive oil while the other ingredients are still mixing. Blend until aioli is smooth and creamy.

To make the roasted red peppers: Place 2 red peppers on a hot grill and blacken the outer skin of the peppers. Place peppers in a bowl and cover with plastic wrap. Once the peppers have softened, peel off the blackened skin and de-seed the peppers under running water. Julienne the peppers and marinate them in a splash of good red wine vinegar and olive oil.

To make the grilled summer vegetables: Go to your local farmers' market and buy a variety of your favorite seasonal vegetables. Preheat grill to medium high. Slice the vegetables ½ inch thick and season with salt and pepper to taste. Toss with extra-virgin olive oil and grill to your liking.

To assemble the sandwiches: Grill the steak to medium-rare or preferred temperature. Let the steak rest 3 to 5 minutes before slicing. While the meat is resting, toast 8 slices of your favorite sandwich bread. Using a spoon or spatula, spread the aioli on the insides of all the bread slices. Place the roasted red peppers and grilled summer vegetables on the bottom part of each slice. Slice the steak against the grain. Place 4 or 5 slices on the red peppers for each sandwich. Close the sandwiches, slice in halves, and serve.

Terra American Bistro

7091 El Cajon Boulevard
San Diego, CA 92115
(619) 293-7088
TERRASD.COM
Owner/Chef: Jeff Rossman

A unique farm-to-table restaurant, Terra American Bistro has a casual atmosphere complete with a tractor garden out front and a wall garden at the entrance. The restaurant is designed with reclaimed materials, including stunning woods, coffee bags covering seat pads, and a captivating chandelier over the chef's communal farm table.

A casual menu boasts flatbread pizzas, Carlsbad mussels, shareable appetizers, salads, and entrees. "We try and use anything local whenever possible, including chicken and pork, and I handpick our fish three to four times per week," says Owner and Chef Jeff Rossman. "A philosophy of sustainability and eating locally is felt strongly by our serving staff, and we take pride in the level of service they provide and the way they educate our guests."

The cuisine at Terra has been labeled as "New American food" with an emphasis on ingredients and preparation styles from North, South, and Central America. Believing that any chef can cook great food, Chef Rossman says he excels at organization, delegation, and motivation. "Being a great chef is also like being a great teacher, mentor, and manager. I love the satisfaction of not only the guests loving the dishes, but also the passion that my servers and back of the house staff take in their work."

Using sustainable, local, and organic ingredients, Chef Rossman has a passion for keeping the environment strong and helping the economy. This philosophy extends to

the bar, which features seasonal fruit and herb-infused vodkas, as well as local craft beers and a wine list that offers more than eighty bottles of mostly California wines.

Chef Rossman's Tuna Tostada with Avocado and Mango Ratatouille recipe was developed and used back in 2003 when the Super Bowl was in San Diego. "I thought it would be cool to have a Thai-inspired dish one year for our Thursday night barbecue," he says.

Tuna Tostada with Avocado & Mango Ratatouille

(SERVES 6–8)

For the mustard seed vinaigrette:

1 cup canola oil
1 tablespoon minced shallots
¼ cup mustard seed
3 tablespoons honey
⅓ cup champagne vinegar
2 tablespoons lemon juice
2 tablespoons white wine
6 tablespoons water
2 tablespoons fresh thyme, finely chopped
Salt and pepper to taste

For the avocado and mango ratatouille:

1 mango, peeled, pit removed, and finely chopped
1 avocado, peeled, pit removed, and finely chopped
¼ teaspoon dry mustard
2 tablespoons lemon juice
3 tablespoons granulated sugar
¼ red onion, minced
Salt and pepper to taste

For the tuna:

2 pounds ahi tuna, sushi grade
2 cups canola oil, for frying
32 gyoza wrappers (round wonton wrappers)
1 head cabbage or romaine, cut into long, thin strips

To make the mustard seed vinaigrette: In a large pan sauté the shallots and mustard seed in the oil until the shallots become translucent and the seeds toast lightly. Transfer shallots and mustard seed to a blender and add the honey, vinegar, lemon juice, white wine, and water. Puree mixture thoroughly, then add the thyme and season with salt and pepper.

To make the avocado and mango ratatouille: Put all ingredients except the salt and pepper in a mixing bowl and combine thoroughly. Season with salt and pepper; reserve.

To prepare the ahi tuna: Finely dice the ahi tuna and toss with the prepared vinaigrette. Heat the oil in a saucepan, fry the gyoza wrappers, and then drain on paper towels. Alternatively, bake the wrappers on a cookie sheet in a preheated 350°F oven for about 15 minutes or until golden brown. Place some of the cabbage or romaine strips on each gyoza wrapper, add a spoonful of the ahi tuna mixture, and then top with some ratatouille.

URBAN SOLACE

3823 30TH STREET
SAN DIEGO, CA 92104
(619) 295-6464
URBANSOLACE.NET
OWNER/CHEF: MATT GORDON

Having a reputation for doing things differently, oftentimes using his menu as an experiment in new flavors and texture combinations, Chef Matt Gordon says he always had a timeline in his head for when he wanted to open a restaurant. "I worked toward that goal for a number of years, gaining experience in a variety of environments to educate myself," he says. "I was a sous chef at twenty-one and an executive chef at twenty-five. I spent the ten years between my first executive chef position getting as much varied experience as I could to cover all facets of truly "owning" a business. Even then, nothing can prepare you for the time and commitment it really requires!"

Owner of both Urban Solace in North Park and its sister restaurant Solace and the Moonlight Lounge in Encinitas, Chef Gordon sources only natural ingredients, even basic

pantry items and bar mixers. "We keep it truly pure, seeking artisan producers for the items we don't make from scratch, and do our best to support small players in the industry when their products are worth highlighting," he says.

Taking nearly a year to completely replace all the typical condiments and other ingredients, you'll now find only homemade sodas and mixers, ketchup, Worcestershire, jams, and jellies in Chef Gordon's restaurants. Chef Gordon also works hard to obtain only the freshest meats and seafood from local sources.

Chef Gordon offers his recipe for Cheese and Chive Biscuits with Orange Honey Butter, saying the biscuits were a memory from a place he worked for a very short time. "We served a biscuit that was so delicious. The flavor stuck in my head for years, so I decided to make my own version." These golden wonders are a staple of Chef Gordon's menus and one of the most popular items, with an equally powerful reputation.

CHEESE & CHIVE BISCUITS
WITH ORANGE HONEY BUTTER

(MAKES 30 BISCUITS)

For the biscuits:

3 cups pastry flour
3 cups all-purpose flour
1½ tablespoons baking powder
2 teaspoons kosher salt
3 sticks unsalted butter
¼ cup minced chives
3 cups white cheddar cheese
1½ cups grated fontina cheese
2½–3 cups buttermilk
Egg whites, whisked (optional)

For the butter:

1 pound unsalted butter
1½ teaspoons grated orange zest
1 tablespoon honey
½ tablespoon kosher salt
½ tablespoon chopped garlic

To make the biscuits: Sift together the flours, baking powder, and salt. Add the butter, chives, and cheeses. Mix with a pastry knife or paddle attachment of a mixer to incorporate the butter. There should still be small chunks of butter; this will make the biscuits flaky. Add the buttermilk and slowly fold together. Do not overmix the dough.

Preheat oven to 400°F.

Place dough on a floured surface and knead two or three times only. Flatten dough out to about a ¾-inch-thickness and cut into desired shapes. Transfer cut biscuits to a baking sheet. Brush the tops with egg whites, if desired, and bake until golden brown, about 12 to 14 minutes.

Chef's note: If you are not using a convection oven, it will probably take a bit longer to cook the biscuits. When the biscuits are golden brown, crack one open to make sure it is cooked inside. If it is not, lower heat to 250°F and check again in a couple of minutes.

To make the butter: Whip butter in a mixer with the whip attachment for 10 minutes, until light and airy. Add remaining ingredients and whip for another 3 minutes. Use immediately, or store in refrigerator but let warm up slightly before using.

THE US GRANT/Grant Grill

326 BROADWAY
SAN DIEGO, CA 92101
(619) 232-3121
USGRANT.NET
EXECUTIVE CHEF: MARK KROPCZYNSKI
DIRECTOR OF VENUES: JEFF JOSENHANS

A true San Diego icon, both THE US GRANT Hotel and the Grant Grill restaurant are more beautiful than any other place in the city. Built in 1910, THE US GRANT was one of the first major hotels built in San Diego, and it has undergone major renovations to celebrate one hundred years of welcoming patrons through their doors. Situated centrally in the historic Gaslamp Quarter, the always-entertaining Horton Plaza is immediately across the street. Guests can experience fine dining in the restaurant or a casual vibe in the lounge, as well as limitless food and beverage options that are perfect for meetings or for events and weddings hosted in one of the ballrooms.

Consistently sourcing the highest-quality ingredients, Executive Chef Mark Kropczynski takes pride in how he runs his banquet kitchen. "All events are treated similar to a dining room experience, versus what one would imagine for a standard hotel banquet," he says. "The food is prepared a la minute, with a focus on freshness and custom menus tailored to the diners' tastes."

Chef Kropczynski says his life as a chef is ever changing and keeps him moving around constantly. As for cooking healthy meals at home, he advises people to enjoy food made from fresh, quality ingredients. "Go ahead: Use butter, cream, and bacon and whatever else you like to eat," he says. "Just eat in moderation, try to exercise regularly, and avoid processed foods."

Passionate about keeping things fresh and local, Chef Kropczynski's recipe for Pan Roasted Duck Breast with Roasted Carnival Squash, Chestnuts, and Dried Apricots is ideal for those cooler weather days. Sommelier, Mixologist, and Director of Venues Jeff Josenhans (left) has created a specialty cocktail that he named the Boisson Bourgogne. Inspired by Burgundy and the fall season, this extraordinary cocktail is a little bitter, a little smoky, and the perfect complement to the pan roasted duck!

PAN ROASTED DUCK BREAST WITH ROASTED CARNIVAL SQUASH, CHESTNUTS & DRIED APRICOTS

(SERVES 4)

For the carnival squash:

1 carnival squash
3 tablespoons honey
2 tablespoons butter
Salt and pepper to taste

For the duck and sauce:

4 duck breasts
1 tablespoon honey
2 tablespoons red wine vinegar
1 cup chicken stock
1 tablespoon butter
Salt and pepper to taste

BOISSON BOURGOGNE COCKTAIL

(serves 1)

1 ounce vodka
1 ounce Dolin red vermouth
1–2 dashes Laphroaig or other Islay scotch
3 ounces California pinot noir
1 ounce Monin Raspberry Syrup
1/4 ounce fresh lemon juice
Cinnamon stick, for garnish

Stir all ingredients in stir glass with ice. Strain into Burgundy glass and garnish with the cinnamon stick.

To plate:

3 dried apricots, julienned
Handful of fresh Italian parsley sprigs, finely chopped

To make the carnival squash: Preheat oven to 325°F.

Cut the squash in half and remove all of the seeds. Place halved squashes onto a sheet pan. Drizzle the honey over the squash and put the butter into the hollowed squash. Bake for approximately 1 to 1½ hours, until soft. Once cooked, peel away the skin of the squash. Place the squash in a bowl and mash until creamy.

To make the duck and sauce: Trim fat from the duck breasts. In an oven-safe frying pan, sear the breasts over medium to high heat (fat side down). Once seared on both sides, finish cooking the breasts in a 400°F oven until medium to medium rare, about 5 minutes. Remove breasts from pan and deglaze the pan with honey. Allow the mixture to boil, then deglaze the pan with vinegar and reduce. Add duck stock and reduce until liquid becomes a sauce consistency. Add the butter and season the sauce with salt and pepper.

To plate: Place mashed squash on a large serving platter. Slice duck breast thinly across the grain of the meat. Serve slices of duck on top of the squash mixture. Drizzle with the duck sauce. Garnish with apricots and parsley.

THE GASLAMP QUARTER

The Gaslamp Quarter is a sixteen-square-block historic district in the center of downtown San Diego. The name comes from the streetlights used in the late 1800s as part of the area's development into a modern city. This area of downtown has quite a colorful history, as it was home to saloons, gambling halls, and bordellos in the late 1800s to early 1900s. It then fell into disrepair and neglect in the mid 1900s. It wasn't until the 1970s that public interest and private investors partnered to redevelop the area as a historic location.

Today the Gaslamp Quarter is the center of shopping, dining, and entertainment, with many original Victorian-era buildings sharing space with modern skyscrapers. Weekend nights are especially vibrant, when the sights and sounds of music and laughter fill the air with energy. Every block brings new choices of cuisine, from the super-fancy to fast casual, and it is the one area of San Diego that remains open until the wee hours of the morning!

VAGABOND KITCHEN

2310 30TH STREET
SOUTH PARK, CA 92104
(619) 255-1035
VAGABONDKITCHEN.COM
OWNER: JEROME GOMBERT
EXECUTIVE CHEF PAUL NILES

With its unique ambiance, high-quality food, and above-average service, Vagabond Kitchen transports diners to a small village restaurant in France. But don't be fooled into thinking that the cuisine is strictly French. Menu items are meant to provide a sample of the best in the world, and the dining room decor is reminiscent of several cultures spanning many continents.

Born and raised in Paris, France, Owner Jerome Gombert is inspired by his travels as well as his love for unique dishes and experiences. "The restaurant has now evolved into a place where using sustainable and local products works well to produce worldly inspired dishes," he says.

For Executive Chef Paul Niles, getting creative with food starts with one ingredient and building from there. "I love having the knowledge that I can use the atmosphere

of the restaurant, and the quality of our food, to help people lose themselves in the experience of dining with us," he says. As well as being a great cook with a passion for what he does, Chef Niles feels his special talent is being able to handle stress when the restaurant is busy. "I work very well when it's packed, and I'm able to deliver under pressure."

Using sustainable, local, and organic ingredients as much as possible, Chef Niles believes that the general public is very aware of what is going on in the food and beverage world. "Creating moments for complete strangers is what I love most about being a chef," he says. "Doing good things for our environment and for our community is the best way to do business. Our recipe for Seafood Bouillabaisse is an interpretation of a classic dish from different parts of the world that has been passed down for generations."

SEAFOOD BOUILLABAISSE

(YIELDS 1 GALLON OR SERVES 4–6)

¼ cup olive oil

2 fennel bulbs, sliced

3 leeks, sliced

10 garlic cloves, sliced

Large pinch saffron

1 tablespoon red pepper flakes

1½ ounces tomato paste

½ cup red wine vinegar

1½ cups white wine

3 pound can whole peeled tomatoes,
    cut into quarters, undrained

2 quarts fish or lobster stock

1 bunch fresh thyme

3 bay leaves

Salt and white pepper to taste

3 lemons, juiced

Seafood of your choice

Crusty baguette, for dipping

In a medium stockpot heat the oil until hot. Add the fennel, leeks, and garlic and simmer slowly. Add the saffron, red pepper flakes, and tomato paste. When the tomato paste has cooked slightly, add the vinegar and white wine and reduce for 2 to 3 minutes. Add the tomatoes and juice, fish or lobster stock, thyme, and bay leaves. Season the bouillabaisse with salt and white pepper, bring to a boil, and then reduce heat to low and simmer for 10 minutes. Add the lemon juice and adjust the seasoning to taste.

Serve bouillabaisse with mussels, clams, shrimp, swordfish, tuna, or sea bass and a crusty baguette for dipping.

Waters Fine Foods & Catering

125 South Highway 101
Solana Beach, CA 92075
(858) 509-9400
waterscatering.com
Owner/Chef: Mary Kay Waters

Making entertaining convenient as well as affordable, Waters Fine Foods & Catering quickly developed a reputation as one of San Diego's top catering companies and has since been consistently named Best Caterer by local media. The edible wonders at this rustic, Napa-style eatery can be enjoyed on the premises, at home, at the office, on a picnic, or during any special event. Walking through the front doors and gazing at the glass cases filled with imaginative and colorful foods make it difficult to choose only one or two items.

Producing distinctive events and providing high-quality local, organic, and sustainable handcrafted fare, Owner Mary Kay Waters has very high standards and takes pride in never taking any short cuts. "I use my classically French–trained techniques as a foundation for all our recipes," she says. "I always use sustainable, local, and organic ingredients. Even our flours, dairy, and nuts are organic."

With locations in San Diego's Bay Park neighborhood and Solana Beach, Chef Waters offers delicious fare for quick, tasty lunches, hors d'oeuvres, gourmet food platters, special holiday meals, and ready-to-serve family dinners. From classic comfort

foods such as chicken pot pies, meatloaf, and enchiladas, to daily selections of freshly made gourmet soups, salads, and sandwiches, Chef Waters likes to keep things simple, buying the best ingredients available and finishing her dishes with flavorful oils. "I like to go for color," she says. "All of those antioxidants and vitamins are good for you!"

When a person's lifestyle includes dining out at restaurants, Chef Waters advises to slow down when eating and really savor all the tastes. "Don't be afraid to ask the kitchen for special requests such as no salt, no dairy, no wheat, whatever your requirements may be." She shares recipes for her ever-popular Butternut Squash Panini and Goat Cheese Mac, two excellent examples of her creativity and utility of fine ingredients.

Butternut Squash Panini

(SERVES 4)

For the butternut squash:

1 butternut squash, peeled and cut into
   ½-inch slices
1 tablespoon olive oil plus more to brush
   on bread and for drizzling
1 tablespoon brown sugar
Salt and pepper to taste

For the sage aioli:

1 cup mayonnaise
1 teaspoon lemon juice
½ teaspoon garlic
6 fresh sage leaves, cut into long thin strips

For assembling the sandwich:

2 slices rosemary bread (or your favorite bread)
8 slices Gruyère cheese
Handful wild arugula
Salt and pepper to taste

To make the butternut squash: Preheat oven to 350°F.

Place squash slices on a baking sheet and brush with 1 tablespoon olive oil. Sprinkle with brown sugar and season with salt and pepper. Bake for 15 to 20 minutes, until golden brown, turning halfway through.

To make the sage aioli: Combine all the ingredients in a blender and puree.

To assemble the sandwich: Preheat griddle over medium-high heat.

For each sandwich, spread sage aioli on one side of one slice of bread. Divide the squash, Gruyère, and wild arugula evenly onto the sage aioli. Drizzle with extra-virgin olive oil and sprinkle with salt and pepper. Spread sage aioli onto one side of the other slice of bread and place on top to form a sandwich. Brush the outsides of the sandwich with olive oil. Grill until golden brown, about 2 minutes each side.

Goat Cheese Mac

(SERVES 8–10)

16 ounces penne pasta

4 tablespoons butter

4 tablespoons flour

4 cups milk

4¼ cups grated firm goat cheese
   (Ariana/Midnight Moon)

¼ cup grated Parmesan cheese

8 ounces fresh soft goat cheese

¼ cup butter (melted)

1 cup panko breadcrumbs

Salt and pepper to taste

Preheat the oven to 375°F.

Fill a large pot with lightly salted water and bring to a boil over high heat. Stir in the penne and cook uncovered, stirring occasionally, until the pasta has cooked through but is still firm to the bite. Drain well.

in a large saucepan over medium heat, melt 4 tablespoons butter; whisk in the flour, stirring 2 to 3 minutes. Slowly add the milk and continue to whisk. Bring mixture to a boil, then turn the heat to a slow simmer, whisking often for approximately 10 minutes.

Add the firm goat cheese, Parmesan, and pasta. Mix well. Place pasta mixture in a large baking dish and dot with soft goat cheese.

Mix ¼ cup melted butter and breadcrumbs in a bowl. Sprinkle the bread crumb mixture evenly over the pasta mixture.

Bake until golden brown on top, about 30 minutes.

WHISKNLADLE

1044 WALL STREET
LA JOLLA, CA 92037
(858) 551-7575
WHISKNLADLE.COM
OWNER/CORPORATE EXECUTIVE CHEF: RYAN JOHNSTON

Whisknladle serves farm-to-table cuisine; think gourmet comfort food infused with Mediterranean influences. The name Whisknladle is based on an underground supper club in Brooklyn. Today Whisknladle Hospitality is the parent company of both Whisknladle and Prepkitchen restaurants. Whisknladle in La Jolla was the first and only restaurant opened in 2008. At present there is a string of Prepkitchen restaurants, including locations in La Jolla, Del Mar, and Little Italy.

Offering his own unique cooking style and distinctive philosophy, Owner and Corporate Executive Chef Ryan Johnston takes an honest back-to-basics approach to dining and doesn't consider himself to be the best cook or the best chef, but he simply loves to cook. "It's my passion that drives me in the kitchen," he says. "Bringing that energy every day sets an example of intensity and a love of food and pure joy."

After being diagnosed with diabetes, Chef Johnston's commitment to working exclusively with quality organic produce that he handpicks from local growers has become a trademark and the focus of his restaurant kitchen. He takes pride and satisfaction in creating a constantly evolving seasonal menu, which highlights fresh local produce and ingredients made from scratch. From baking bread and making pasta, to curing and aging meats, and even churning his own ice cream, Chef Johnston ensures everything is made in-house.

Popular favorites at the restaurants include Radiatori with Milk Braised Lamb Shoulder, Swiss Chard, and Salsa Verde and Beer

Braised Beef with Celery Root Mash and Gremolota. "I love both dishes because they touch my soul," says Chef Johnston. "The lamb pasta is the more sophisticated dish, and the flavors are more dynamic. It's a dish that makes me feel like I am in the hills of Verona or Tuscany on vacation. The braised beef is more of an 'everyday meal,' something my grandmother would make. Hers was less complicated but just as delicious."

RADIATORI WITH MILK BRAISED LAMB SHOULDER, SWISS CHARD & SALSA VERDE

(SERVES 4)

For the lamb:

4 pounds boneless lamb shoulder

Salt and pepper to taste

¼ cup (½ stick) butter

2 cups canola oil

1 tablespoon crushed garlic

2 tablespoons fresh and lightly chopped marjoram

Juice of 1 lemon

1 quart milk

3 tablespoons kosher salt

For the salsa verde:

1 tablespoon crushed garlic

1 salted anchovy, rinsed and smashed in mortar

2 tablespoons Cabernet vinegar

1 teaspoon Dijon mustard

2 teaspoons capers, finely chopped

3 tablespoons finely chopped fresh basil

3 tablespoons finely chopped parsley

3 tablespoons finely chopped mint

¾ cups extra-virgin olive oil

For the swiss chard:

9 pounds (16 bunches) Swiss chard, washed and
　separated from stems

2 tablespoons peeled and minced garlic

2 tablespoons peeled and finely diced shallots

For plating:

1 pound radiatori pasta

½ cup cream

¼ cup grated Parmigiana Reggiano

To make the lamb: Before braising the lamb, cut it into 1-inch cubes, sprinkle with salt and pepper, and allow to rest, covered in the refrigerator, overnight.

The following day preheat the oven to 300°F. Heat butter and oil together in a heavy-bottomed Dutch oven or braising pan. When hot, pan sear the lamb cubes in batches, letting each side get nicely caramelized (brown); set aside.

Once all the meat has been seared, drain the majority of the oil out of the pan and add the garlic, marjoram, and lemon juice; sauté until fragrant.

Add the lamb back into the pan. Then add the milk, bringing it to a simmer. Once the milk is simmering, cover the pan and place it in the oven until the lamb is tender, approximately 2 hours.

To make the salsa verde: While the lamb is braising, combine the garlic, anchovy, vinegar, Dijon mustard, and capers in a small bowl. Add the basil, parsley, mint, and oil and mix again, being careful not to bruise the herbs. Set aside.

To make the Swiss chard: Roughly chop the Swiss chard and dice the stems into small portions, keeping the greens and the stems separate for now. Bring lightly salted water to a boil in a large pot. Blanch the stems for approximately 90 seconds, until tender. Remove and cool the stems in an ice bath. Repeat this step with the greens, blanching for 60 seconds and then moving to an ice bath to cool.

In a medium-size pot over low heat, cook the garlic and shallots until completely soft. Then add the stems and sauté. Finally, add the greens and braise for approximately 7 minutes. Set aside.

To plate: In a large pot boil some salted water and add in the pasta. Allow to cook for approximately 6 to 10 minutes, until al dente.

To pull the dish together, in a large bowl combine the lamb, lamb juices, pasta, Swiss chard, and cream. Season with salt and pepper to taste.

Spread the mixture evenly in a large casserole dish and sprinkle Parmesan cheese evenly over the mixture.

Put the casserole dish on a sheet pan and bake in a 450°F oven for 10 minutes, until cheese is golden brown.

Allow to cool for 5 minutes, then serve family style. Enjoy!

Beer Braised Beef with Celery Root Mash & Gremolata

(SERVES 4)

For the braised beef:

½ cup canola oil

4 pounds boneless short ribs, seasoned overnight

½ cup finely diced carrots

½ cup finely diced yellow onions

½ cup finely diced celery

¼ cup dark brown sugar

1 tablespoon Dijon mustard

¼ cup tomato paste

1 bottle porter beer

1 quart veal beef stock

½ quart chicken stock

For the celery root mash:

¼ cup butter

2 pounds celery root, peeled and cut into large dice

1¼ pounds gala apples, peeled, cored, and cut into large dice

1 garlic clove

1 bay leaf

3 cups heavy cream

For the gremolata:

½ cup washed and roughly chopped parsley

¼ cup peeled and finely chopped garlic

3 lemons, zested

For the braised beef: Preheat oven to 300° F. Heat oil in a large sauté pan. When oil is hot, pan sear the short ribs, letting each side get a nice brown caramelization; set aside in a large baking pan.

In the same sauté pan, add the carrots, onions, and celery and cook on low heat until soft and tender. Mix in the brown sugar, mustard, and tomato paste. Cook for 1 minute.

Deglaze the sauté pan with the beer and leave to reduce until the alcohol has been cooked out, approximately 5 minutes. Then add both the beef and chicken stock. Bring the mixture to a boil and then pour it over the beef.

Place parchment paper on top of the beef in the baking pan and cook until tender, approximately 2½ hours.

For the celery root mash: When the meat is nearly finished, begin cooking the celery root mash. In a medium-size saucepan, combine the butter, celery root, apples, garlic, and bay leaf and slowly cook over a low heat.

Once the apples and celery root are tender and completely cooked, add the cream and cover, cooking until it has reduced by half.

Remove from heat and carefully take out the bay leaf. Puree the mixture in a food processor or blender until smooth. Season with salt to taste.

For the gremolata: Mix the gremolata ingredients together in a small bowl; set aside.

To plate: Divide the celery root mash among four serving plates and top with braised beef, topping with juices from the pan and gremolata. Or, serve side by side with a vegetable of your choice.

THE WINE PUB

2907 SHELTER ISLAND DRIVE
SAN DIEGO, CA 92106
(619) 758-9325
THEWINEPUBSD.COM
OWNER: SANDY HANSHAW
EXECUTIVE CHEF: MALISSA SORSBY

At The Wine Pub, think handpicked wines, handcrafted foods, and Point Loma flavor! "This is not just our tagline, but also the way we live at The Pub," says owner Sandy Hanshaw. "Everything on our menu is carefully selected to reflect the unique tastes of our neighborhood."

What started out as a wine bar with a small menu has developed into a wine and beer bar serving a menu of artisan-style food, including small plates to full entrees.

From unique wines to vegan, vegetarian, and full gluten-free options, The Wine Pub is dedicated to meeting anyone's dietary needs. "The food has become a much bigger part of the plan than originally anticipated," says Executive Chef Malissa Sorsby. "The Wine Pub thrives on offering something out of the ordinary—different, yet still comfortable."

The Stuffed Portobellinis are a great showcase for some fabulous ingredients such as homemade bread crumbs, fresh sage, artichoke hearts, and fresh apple. They all meld together in such a great way to create a delicious little melting pot in each mushroom. "This is one of my favorite items to share with newcomers to The Pub," says Chef Sorsby. "It's slow roasted to bring out all the flavors, and it pairs wonderfully with our Sean Minor Pinot Noir. It's a great way to highlight our attention to quality."

A favorite among diners, the Banana Caramel Bread Pudding recipe has been altered numerous times to create perfectly caramelized bananas and a well-balanced custard. "This is one item that gets the whole staff excited," Chef Sorsby says. "When they smell the bananas and caramel, everyone becomes a quality-control expert. Personally I love this recipe because, although it is a heavier dessert and perfect for the chilly months, it's light enough to enjoy on a warm summer night on the patio with a glass of muscat."

STUFFED PORTOBELLINIS

(SERVES 8–10)

1 cup whole-milk ricotta cheese
¼ pound Italian sausage, cooked and chopped
¼ cup chives
½ cup artichoke hearts
1 Granny Smith apple, cut into small dice
1 cup homemade bread crumbs
½ cup grated Parmesan cheese
Handful fresh sage, chopped, to taste
Salt and pepper to taste
8–10 portobellini mushrooms, cleaned and
    stems removed
Extra-virgin olive oil, for drizzling

Preheat oven to 350°F.

Combine all the ingredients except the mushrooms and olive oil in a large bowl and mix well to combine.

Stuff mushrooms and place on a large baking sheet. Drizzle with olive oil and bake for 30 minutes, until mushrooms are cooked thoroughly and stuffing starts to turn golden brown. Chef Sorsby recommends serving the mushrooms with a balsamic vinegar reduction (equal parts sugar and balsamic vinegar).

Banana Caramel Bread Pudding

(SERVES 6–8)

For the custard:

9 eggs

1 cup granulated sugar

1½ cups whole milk

1½ tablespoons vanilla

2 cups heavy cream

1½ ciabatta loaves (or your favorite bread),
    cut into 1 x 1-inch cubes

For the banana caramel:

1 cup sugar

1 tablespoon water

3 tablespoons butter

1 tablespoon lemon juice

7 medium-size bananas (approximately 2 pounds),
    peeled and sliced

Caramel ice cream (or your favorite flavor)

For the custard: In a large mixing bowl, whisk the eggs until fluffy. Add the sugar and whisk until well combined. Add the milk, vanilla, and cream and whisk thoroughly. Toss the bread into the custard mixture and coat evenly. Refrigerate for at least 1 hour.

For the banana caramel: In a large saucepan mix together the sugar and water and cook over medium heat until caramel starts to form. Add butter slowly and stir to combine. Turn heat to medium-low and then add the lemon juice and bananas. Cook for 3 to 4 minutes.

Preheat oven to 350°F.

Coat a large casserole dish with nonstick cooking spray. Layer half of the bread-custard mixture into the bottom of the dish, followed by half of the banana-caramel mixture. Finish with the other half of the bread-custard mixture and then evenly cover the top with the remaining banana-caramel mixture.

Bake the bread pudding until golden brown, approximately 1 hour. Allow to set for 10 minutes and then serve warm with caramel ice cream.

SOCIAL DINING EXPERIENCE

A local icon with the rare opportunity to play in a national spotlight, Brian Malarkey is both proud and humbled by his rise in the culinary world. As a contestant in Bravo's hit show *Top Chef Miami,* Malarkey gained attention for his off-beat style, electric smile, and unique head-wear. Landing the role as a celebrity judge in ABC's *The Taste* (the culinary equivalent of *American Idol* and *The Voice*) has vaulted him into a level rarely achieved by any Chef.

No doubt that Malarkey has the golden touch. Just gaze at his current collection of San Diego-based restaurants, centered around the concept of providing a "Social Dining Experience," akin to a large dinner party with upbeat music, comfortable open spaces, high-quality food, and uniquely-crafted cocktails. Searsucker was his first business venture, buzzing in the center of the Gaslamp Quarter in downtown. Del Mar is home to Burlap, his take on "Asian Cowboy" cuisine. Herringbone is a bright and airy addition to the La Jolla community, serving "Ocean Bazaar" cuisine. Located in the Point Loma area, Gabardine is a popular neighborhood kitchen. In the southeast community of La Mesa you will find the "urban cowboy diner" named Gingham.

He also owns a successful catering business in San Diego, and is collaborating with partner James Brennan to open other dining establishments across the U.S.

THE WINESELLER & BRASSERIE

9550 WAPLES STREET
SAN DIEGO, CA 92121
(858) 450-9557
WINESELLAR.COM
OWNER: GARY PARKER

Opened in Sorrento Mesa in November 1988, the distinctive WineSeller & Brasserie is a cut above the rest. The wine shop offers wine-storage facilities located in the center of the populated county, housed in a tall building to facilitate the structure of the locker design. They also specialize in and offer rare and fine wines in both The WineSeller & Brasserie.

"We found that renting wine lockers to people was an excellent resource for accessing bottled vintage gems that people needed to sell for various reasons. I would appraise the private collections and purchase or broker the cellars for the locker renters," says Owner Gary Parker. "Through this I accumulated an amazing lineup of rare and fine wines that earned the Wine Spectator Grand Award every year we have been open. For many of our twenty-four years we were the lone San Diego restaurant to hold this award. Only seventy-five restaurants on the planet currently hold this honor."

Having an affinity for contemporary French cuisine, Parker started off less formal as far as the menu and interior design went, but the wine list and the quality of the food dictated that the chef take more care in his presentations. "We did this and were consistently rated in Zagat San Diego as either the best or one of the top three restaurants for quality of food," Parker says. "We also love doing wine-theme dinners, special wine tastings, and wine and food pairings and having special wine sales. We now have three wine-of-the-month wine clubs."

The size of the space has doubled over the years, and Parker has added a private dining room for meetings and special events and recently added a bar in the wine shop called The Casual Side. "Here we feature happy hour food and drink, along with craft beer selections on tap," he says. "Today we are still considered a special-occasion restaurant by many people and have been serving some clients every year as they celebrate weddings and anniversaries. We also find ourselves serving the local community of businesses, providing people with an excellent place to meet and do business, without having to worry about the food, service, or atmosphere."

Following, the restaurant shares one of their most popular and long-standing items on their menu, pairing two unlikely partners in a single dish with outstanding results.

Pan Roasted Scallops Pork Belly Bourguignon with Glazed Vegetables & Chives

(SERVES 6)

2 pounds pork belly, cut into 1½-inch pieces

Salt and pepper to taste

¼ cup olive oil

4 brown onions, peeled and sliced

2 tablespoons all-purpose flour

1 cup really good white Burgundy

4 large carrots, chopped

2 garlic cloves, finely chopped

2 sprigs thyme

2 bay leaves

1 sprig rosemary

12 U10 scallops

Canola oil, for frying scallops

2 bunches green onions, finely chopped, for garnish

Season pork with salt and pepper. In a large Dutch oven or oven-safe saucepan, heat oil over high heat and add the pork in small batches, searing the pork on all sides until browned.

When all the pork is browned, add onions and turn down the heat to medium, cooking the onions until soft, about 8 minutes. Sprinkle the flour over the pork and onions and cook, stirring constantly, for about 4 minutes.

Remove the pork-onion mixture and place in a large bowl. Add wine to the saucepan and scrape all the little bits from the bottom. Bring the wine to a boil, then return the pork and carrots to the pan along with the garlic, thyme, bay leaves, and rosemary. Add just enough water to cover the pork and place lid on the pan.

Preheat oven to 300°F. Cook pork in the oven for about 2½ to 3 hours, checking every hour, until pork is fork-tender.

Lightly season the scallops with salt and pepper. In a large frying pan coated with canola oil over medium-high heat, sear 6 scallops at a time, for about 2 minutes on each side, until golden. Place the scallops on a baking sheet and cook in the oven for about 2 minutes.

Evenly distribute the Pork Belly Bourguignon and vegetables among six bowls. Place 2 scallops in each bowl and garnish with green onions.

Recipe Index

General Index

About the Author

Maria Desiderata Montana is the publisher of the award-winning food blog San Diego Food Finds (sandiegofoodfinds.com). She is also a published author, editor, and award-winning freelance food and wine journalist who learned how to cook and appreciate European cuisine from her parents, who were born and raised in Calabria, Italy. Maria is the author of Food Lovers' Guide to San Diego (Globe Pequot Press) and The Inn at Rancho Santa Fe Cookbook. She was also a contributing editor of the award-winning cookbook *Flying Pans.* She is extensively published in several newspapers and magazines, where she has written a variety of food and entertainment stories, as well as her own monthly "Step by Step" recipe series. Maria loves to cook and create new recipes and strongly believes that eating with family and friends is a celebration of life itself. She lives in San Diego with her husband, John, and their two children, Lucia and Frank.

About the Photographer

John Dole has been photographing professionally for the past ten years in the greater San Diego area. In that time he has shot anything from portraits to food to architecture. His love of cuisine and photography made this project a dream come true and he was elated to be a part of it. A big fan of aesthetics, the dishes prepared for this book made a perfect subject for him as every dish was looked upon as a piece of art.

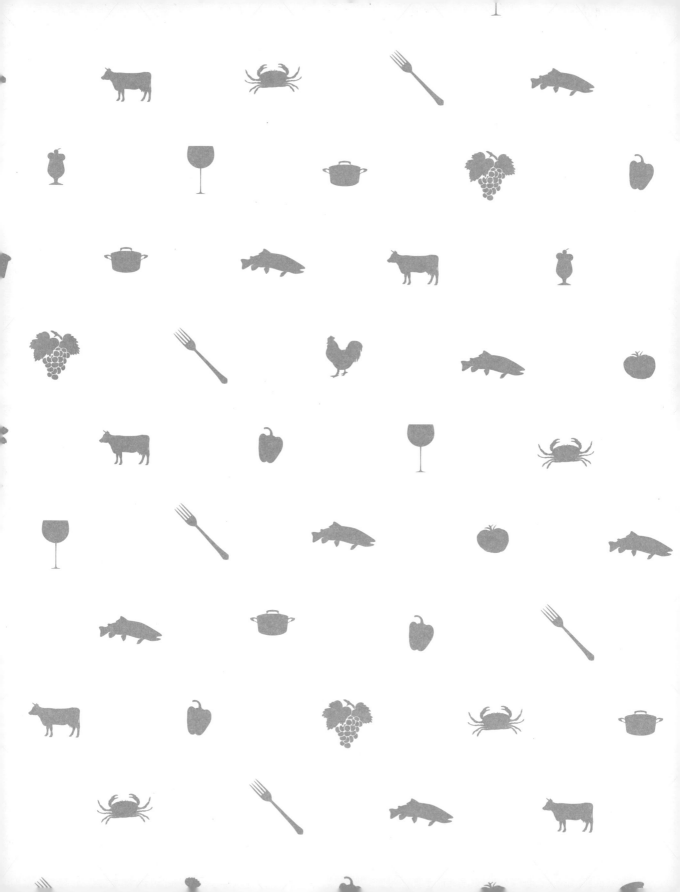